Schnitzer
O'Shea

Schnitzer O'Shea

Donall MacAmhlaidh

BRANDON

First published in 1985
Brandon Book Publishers Ltd.
Dingle, Co. Kerry, Ireland
and 51 Washington Street,
Dover, New Hampshire 03820, U.S.A.

MacAmhlaidh, Donall
    Schnitzer O'Shea.
    I. Title
    823'.914[F] PR6063.A117/

    ISBN 0-86322-079-7

This book is published with the assistance of the Arts Council (An Chomhairle Ealaíon).
The author is grateful to East Midland Arts for the bursary which enabled him to devote time
to this work.
A shorter and different version of this book was published in Irish by An Clóchomhar in
1974.

Cover design by Brendan Foreman
Typeset by Setleaders Limited, Dublin
Printed by Billings Limited, England

To Maureen, for all her help

✿✿ Chapter One. ✿✿

SCHNITZER THEOPHILUS O'SHEA was born in Wigan, Lancashire, and not as is commonly believed in the Co Kilkenny townland of Muldowneyscourt in the barony of Glenbeg where he grew up. Schnitzer's mother, Honoria Brophy-Grace, came home from England after an absence of two or three years with an infant son, an imitation wedding ring and no evidence at all, photographic or documentary, that she had ever been joined in holy wedlock. Nor even that she had recoursed to a registry office ceremony as some girls in her predicament might do! There was talk of course, but Honoria was singularly guarded and eventually the curiosity of the neighbourhood withered and died from the same lack of information that had first inspired it. Who Schnitzer's father was, where he hailed from, what trade or profession he followed: Honoria met all such questions with a smile of such profound inscrutability as to discourage the most presumptuous inquisitor.

That the poet's father was a Munsterman is possible, given the prevalence of the surname in Cork and Kerry, and he may well have been a navvy or seaman whose footloose disposition made him reluctant to embrace the responsibilities of the married state. And we can only speculate as to why Honoria encumbered her son with such outlandish Christian names. It was only after she had gone into domestic service in England that Honoria adopted her mother's maiden name of Brophy as a prefix to her own. It may be that she picked her baby's names from some comic cut or woman's magazine (her literary tastes were of this nature) or that she heard them somewhere and liked the sound of them. If so it was a preference which her son did not share, being embarrassed in particular by his second name, Theophilus. Hiram S. Walbark, the poet's American biographer, confidently deduces German or Austrian paternity from the name Schnitzer; a faulty inference surely for O'Shea's facial characteristics were strikingly Irish.

Schnitzer O'Shea was reared by his aged and widowed

7

grandfather Turlough Grace, the task falling to the old man when his daughter Honoria took off with a soldier from the military barracks in Kilkenny without as much as a word to anyone. Honoria and the deserter went to England, it is believed, but the liaison can't have lasted very long for a few years later Honoria was working in a shabby little eating place in the Bronx, an establishment called Eddie's Eats if the information is correct. Hiram S. Walbark is of the opinion that Honoria married an American serviceman stationed in Britain and thus gained entry to the United States; a plausible enough supposition but, in the absence of proof, nothing more. It was a man by the name of Brennan from the townland of Skeoughmore* who wrote home to say that he had spoken to Honie Grace, as she was known locally, and that she had affected not to know him even though they had grown up in the same parish. Honoria's consort now was a Puerto Rican whom the Skeoughmore man uncharitably described as being as big as a camel and twice as ugly: the Puerto Rican, it seems, resented Brennan's familiarity with Honoria and the two were about to come to blows when an Irish-American policeman intervened to arrest the black man. It was at this stage, according to Brennan, that Honoria abandoned her pretence and began abusing her compatriot in the most deplorable language as she sought to obstruct the police officer in the execution of his duty. Nothing more was heard of Honoria Brophy-Grace and Schnitzer grew up with no recollection at all of his mother, a deprivation for which he was seemingly none the worse.

Turlough Grace was a landless cottager if we discount the acre of ground that went with the rented dwelling and on which he cultivated potatoes and cabbage. As mere cottagers the Graces were at the bottom of the rural social structure, without even a claim to respectability since Honoria's transgression in bringing Schnitzer Theophilus into the world. The Graces' livestock consisted of two goats tethered to a spike at the bottom of the garden or permitted to hobble, spancelled,

*A barbarous anglicisation of Sceach Mhór or Big Bush. Irish placenames were subjected to atrocious corruptions under English rule and nowadays there is a disturbing tendency to use the English translation. Even "Skeoughmore" is preferable to "Big Bush".

along the quiet roads of Glenbeg. In a farming community this lack of kine (to borrow the phrase of another Irish poet of stature) was a badge of poverty, a disqualification which O'Shea would have cast up at him on one very particular occasion in years to come.

By all accounts Schnitzer O'Shea was a very ordinary little boy, giving no hint at all of the literary gifts which were to blossom so startlingly in later years. Primary–school teacher Peter McGilligan writing in The Rod, that now-defunct organ of the teaching profession in Ireland, said that of all the pupils he put through his hands in the course of a long and dedicated career none showed less sign of literary promise than little Schnitzer. Indeed, Mr McGilligan has often spoken with bitterness of his pupil's failure to give any sign, however small, of his latent talent, his future greatness: if there were only an anecdote or two or some significant little incident to recount when people asked him about the schooldays of the famous poet! But no, the retired teacher told us aggrievedly over a drink in Podge Maher's Bar & Grocery in Muldowneyscourt, O'Shea was so ordinary as to be damn near invisible. "In fact," Mr McGilligan confided with a sudden flash of rancour, "I can hardly remember the little bastard at all!"

It would be incorrect, just the same, to say that Schnitzer gave no indication at all of his poetic bent while still at school. Teachers can be as unaware of their charges' talents as the children themselves may be ignorant of their teachers' virtues: in fact Schnitzer O'Shea had begun to string lines of verse together while still at school; simple little quatrains like the following:

There was Flukey Walsh and Snuffy Dunne
And Tom and Johnny Scanlon,
Mick and Dick and Blinky Gunn
And limping Paddy Hanlon . . .

These few lines of schoolboy doggerel would hardly justify great expectations, to be sure, but mighty oaks from tiny acorns grow and although Schnitzer O'Shea's passage through the Muldowneyscourt National School was far from spectacular he had gained a reputation locally as a poet while still in his teens. Old issues of the Kilkenny People and the Kilkenny Journal contain many examples of his work; undistinguished verse in the traditional ballad mode so popular then in country districts, and all of it in English. It was not until after he emigrated to Britain, oddly enough, that Schnitzer began to write entirely in Irish.

Schnitzer O'Shea left school at thirteen, the legally permissible age in those days, so as to be of help to his grandfather then fast approaching his end. Turlough Cuffe* Grace was reputedly the last native Irish speaker in the barony of Glenbeg and it was from him that Schnitzer acquired his excellent command of the language. What little Irish Schnitzer – or for that matter any of Peter McGilligan's pupils – learned at school could be comfortably accommodated on the back of a postage stamp, as the teacher himself ruefully admitted in that article which he wrote for *The Rod*. O'Shea's publishers substantiate this: the poet's syntax could be very unorthodox and he never yielded to the modern standardised spelling. What is remarkable, not to say fortuitous, is the manner in which the boy picked up the language from old Turlough who had not spoken it for many years, not even to his daughter Honoria when she was a child. For it was through some strange quirk of oncoming dotage (hastened possibly by the traumatic experience of being left to look after his grandson) that the old man reverted to the language of his youth, refusing stubbornly to communicate with anyone in English which had long been the vernacular of Glenbeg. And so it was that Schnitzer had no choice but to grow up speaking Irish in its most idiomatic and racy form, the more so since his grandfather grew in-

---

The incongruity of the name Cuffe has a ready explanation: the Cuffe-Graingers were landed gentry who occupied their ancestral demesne at the southern extremity of the barony of Glenbeg. They were held in great esteem and affection by the country-folk because of their humane treatment of their tenants and employees – a rare enough thing in those days – and it was not unusual for the peasantry to name children after them. Dr Dáithí Ó Bógáin, the noted folklorist, in his erudite study The Gaelic of Glenbeg includes a fine lament in Irish for one member of this family, the Rt Hon Barnabus Cuffe-Grainger, MP, who represented Kilkenny at Westminster for more than a quarter of a century and who had the distinction of delivering the longest maiden speech ever heard in the House of Commons; an impassioned plea for the curtailment of the canine species by means of a dog licence. He was also an accomplished tin-whistle player and could dance a jig, it was said, on a china platter without breaking it! Barnabus had a passion for the ancient game of hurling and did all he could to foster it, often taking part in the game himself, long before the Gaelic Athletic Association came into being. Not all the Anglo-Irish landlords were callous despots, it must be said.

creasingly loquacious with age and would hold forth for hours on end – even when there was nobody present – on matters of remote or immediate interest. With the sole honourable exception of Dr Ó Bógáin it has to be said that Gaelic Revivalists failed miserably to avail of this godsent opportunity to record for posterity the priceless verbal heritage that was squandered so prodigally in the labourer's cottage in Glenbeg. Obsessed with the Irish speakers of the western seaboard they neglected this last repository of Leinster Irish that lay only a few hours' drive from Dublin. Dr Ó Bógáin alone visited Turlough Grace and tape-recorded leagues of precious verbiage, folklore in prose and verse, recollections and observations on life in the barony and much else. On the occasions when Schnitzer was present he contributed little or nothing to the proceedings and Ó Bógáin, like Peter McGilligan, confessed that he never credited the grandson with poetic ability.

A COUPLE of years after Schnitzer left school Turlough Grace died and Schnitzer, relinquishing all claim to the cottage, went to work for a local farmer, Mr Fintan Bolger of Dromawn Aneerin, at a wage that was meagre enough even by the standards of the day. Seventeen shillings a week, fed and found, was Schnitzer's pay as a farm-labourer and he earned every penny of it many times over. Fintan Bolger was not an unkindly man but he was the product of a hard up-bringing and it seemed right and proper to him that a hired man should be underpaid and overworked: he himself wasn't in the least averse to hard work and long hours; in fact he subscribed to the belief that long hours of hard work were beneficial to man and beast alike. What, he would enquire of Schnitzer, could be more damaging to the spirit than to spend your waking hours propping up the street corners like those useless yokes inside in the town? Hadn't the Man Above decreed that we must earn our bread by the sweat of our brow, and what better authority could you ask than that?

But harsh conditions apart Schnitzer O'Shea was tolerably satisfied in his employment, and if the job left something to be desired in the way of status or remuneration it was preferable to an orphanage or industrial school where the young inmates were sometimes rumoured to be less than happy. There was always enough to eat – good wholesome fare – in the Bolger household and a clean bed of straw in the loft for the servant boy. Mary Ellen Bolger, the farmer's wife, was a kindly soul and she furthered Schnitzer's education somewhat by supplying him with reading material to beguile the long winter nights, a copy of *Ireland's Own* or *The Lantern* or the ubiquitous *Old Moore's Almanack*. This latter publication fascinated Schnitzer and he would greedily absorb the many nuggets of information it contained; lighting-up time in Belfast or Cardiff, the phases of the moon or high-water time in the various ports of Ireland and Britain. Schnitzer would pore over the *Almanack* for hours on end with all the absorption of a young Muslim studying the Koran, and he possessed so remarkable a memory that he forgot almost nothing of what he read. This gift of the poet's was to evoke a great deal of comment in the years ahead and it says little for Mr McGilligan's qualities as a teacher that he failed to notice O'Shea's great powers of retention. One can only wonder how the boy might have fared under a more perceptive tutor!

There was an old dictionary in the Bolger household too and Schnitzer would often immerse himself in its pages, hunting down unfamiliar words with all the persistence of a beagle. Mary Ellen recalls him sitting at the kitchen table by the light of the paraffin lamp (this was before the boon of rural electrification had penetrated the barony of Glenbeg) with his finger running eagerly down through the columns of small print and his tongue protruding with "the dint of concentration". The poet's early education, patchy as it was, owed more to those winter nights in Mary Ellen's kitchen than to all the days he spent at school and it may well be that in the young labourer's studiousness the good woman saw some promise of the fulfilment that lay ahead.

As time went on Schnitzer's great love of words, their sound and meaning – their very *texture*, one might say – began to manifest itself more and more. He would, for instance, take a shine to some word or phrase which he had seen in print or heard in the cinema and then that word or phrase would be on his lips night and day until it became meaningless from sheer repetition, a bone sucked dry of its last morsel of marrow. Exotic words and expressions held a special magic for the

12

budding poet, sustaining and nourishing him almost as much as the food he ate; his pet words were juicy mouthfuls which he savoured to the full, thrilled by their power of evocation, the wonderful images they created. *Copacabana*, Schnitzer would murmur softly as he worked his way through a drill of sugar-beet, yanking the stubborn roots from the soil . . . *Copacabana* he would whisper reverentially, and the rain-drenched Irish countryside all round would dissolve into a Hollywood film set . . . *Copacabana*, he would intone ecstatically and be transported to a moonlit patio beneath a sky that glittered with stars, a dark-eyed *señorita* by his side and the air vibrant with strumming guitars . . . *Copa-cabana*, he would chant druidically, and then *Co-pa-ca-ba-na*, exploring each permutation until it seemed to him that the word was a verbal kaleidoscope yielding endless variations . . . *Cop-aca-bana* he would breathe, lost to the world about him.

Placenames with romantic connotations appealed irresistibly to Schnitzer's imagination, Kamchatka and Bali and Vienna and Saskatchewan to name but a few. Saskatchewan in particular captivated the young poet with its strange allure. *Saskatchewan* he would declaim a thousand times a day . . . *Sas-kat-che-wan*, inaudibly, until the spell was complete and he was no longer grubbing for potatoes in the damp soil or forking dung in Bolger's farmyard, but gazing enraptured at the boundless prairie and sky, or a mountain lake girth round by the snow-capped Rockies. Or again he might yell *Saskatchewan!* at the melancholy Irish sky, squandering the vast wealth of the word in one reckless fling . . . *Saskatchewan!* he would cry and in place of the ragged hedges and the unkempt Irish landscape there would spread before him the panoramic splendour of the Canadian West, the waving wheatfields stretching to the horizon's rim, the fragrant pine woods, the timeless Rockies. Thus did the young Schnitzer ameliorate the drudgery of the farmworker's life, cocooning himself against reality in the mystical power of words.

Like most of his generation Schnitzer was an enthusiastic picture-goer and after he had bought an old army bike for a pound at an auction in Kilkenny he thought nothing at all of cycling the ten miles or so several nights a week to visit the cinema. The cinema opened up the great wide world beyond Glenbeg more graphically than the most devoted attention to books could have ever done: it was all there before him on the silver screen and from the hard wooden seats in the fourpenny place he devoured it with avid eyes; the fairyland skyline of Manhattan, the golden beaches of Hawaii, the human anthill of Hong Kong. With the fresh receptivity of youth Schnitzer entered wholeheartedly into the glamorous world of celluloid and he lived the roles he saw enacted there for days after, sneering like Humphrey Bogart at some hoodlum's threat or laughing with insolent courage like Errol Flynn when faced with danger; even forgetting himself so far, on occasion, as to startle someone with a scowl or a grimace the origin of which they could never have guessed. The screen-struck youngster was more characteristic of town than of country life and Schnitzer's little excursions into the realms of fantasy were bound to be misunderstood by the people among whom he lived, thus it is not entirely surprising that he came to have a reputation for eccentricity.

For the young man the charm of the cinema was aural as well as visible. There were new words to be heard, alluring placenames, grandiloquent idioms and catchy American expressions. Which is not to say that he preferred the foreign or the outlandish to what was native and Irish, for there were old familiar placenames like Skeoughvostheen and Gragara and Templeorum that enthralled him with their mellifluous or rhythmical quality. *Gragara,* he would murmur, accenting the final vowel heavily . . . *Gragara,* moving the emphasis back to the middle of the word . . . *Gragara,* he would croon, altering the stress yet again as though seeking a pronunciation that would unlock some hidden meaning just as the magic word "Sesame" had unlocked the robbers' cave in the Ali Baba story. It was the same with Clashganny or Tubbergurlick or Boher-a-townish. The names of these obscure townlands delighted the young poet every bit as much as Mandalay or Valparaiso or even Guadeloupe, and he drained each in turn of their strange appeal. And one year he learned a new placename that bewitched him like a precious stone: it happened when a *spailpín** passed through the district and

* *Anglicised as spalpeen, an itinerant farm labourer hired out seasonally. The word had pejorative overtones in Victorian times, often being used as a derogatory term for an Irishman.*

14

hired out for a few weeks to a farmer called Ned Purcell in the parish of Skeoughmore. The *spailpín*, a native of Connemara, had only a rudimentary acquaintance with the English language and he was gratified to find in Schnitzer O'Shea someone with whom he could chew the rag, so to speak, in his mother tongue – even if, as he was later to remark, the Muldowneyscourt man spoke an unfamiliar dialect thick with archaic expressions and quaint turns of phrase! The *spailpín* told Schnitzer that he came from a place called Lettermuckoo[*] and the name exercised such a fascination over Schnitzer that he would repeat it, tremulous with wonder, a thousand times a day. *Lettermuckoo*, he would murmur, conjuring up a vision of bogland and mountain, *Lettermuckoo*, he'd whisper raptly . . . *Let-ter-muck-oo*; and then with gathering speed, in an abandon of vocal delight, *Lettermuckoo-Lettermuckoo-Lettermuckoo-Lettermuckooooooo*! rising to a shrill crescendo if there was no one about. Schnitzer was thus occupied one day when Fintan Bolger came upon him unexpectedly in the lower end of a meadow where he was widening a drain and after a momentary hesitation the farmer asked what ailed him or why was he making such strange sounds? Somewhat abashed, Schnitzer denied that anything at all ailed him but when the farmer pressed him for an explanation he admitted that he sometimes talked to himself.

"Sure I suppose," he added a mite defensively, "everyone has his own little ways."

"Begor boy, I suppose they have," the farmer conceded and walked off. Some time later, however, he recounted the experience to a couple of his cronies over a drink in Podge Maher's pub and Lar Buggy, a small hill-farmer from over Knockeven way, expressed his belief that the lad was unbalanced and that only a half-eejit, as he put it, would behave in that manner, mouthing strange words to himself when he thought there was nobody listening. That kind of carry-on couldn't be tolerated at all, Lar Buggy declared, for you'd never know what it might lead to.

[*] *Litir Mochua in Irish, the Hillside of Mochua. St Mochua was one of the great luminaries of Ireland's Golden Age when learning and piety shone like a beacon of salvation for pagan Europe. Again one must deplore the barbarism of the anglicised form: "Lettermuckoo" is a travesty.*

"And 'tis not off the wind he took it, either," put in 'Más Delaney. "Sure didn't his oul grandfather take the same figgery, talking to himself to bate the divil below in the house and nobody there at all half of the time?"

"And who knows what nature is in him beside that, sure what does anyone know about the other half of him? His father could be a Chinaman for all we know," Lar Buggy suggested. "I'd get rid of him, Bolger, if I was you, for it isn't known what the likes of him would do if he took the notion!"

"Begor he done nothing out of the way so far," Fintan Bolger replied, loyally defending his employee. "Damn the bit of trouble he gave me since the day he came to me!"

"And ain't there always a first time?" asked 'Más Delaney between puffs at his pipe. "Wouldn't it be a nice how-do-you-do if he set fire to the house on you some night, or if he got up and murdered ye all in ye're beds?"

"There's a fear of him!" declared Fintan Bolger with conviction.

"Well I'd not have the likes of him about the place at all, so I wouldn't," Lar Buggy insisted and it was at this juncture that another customer, a rate collector by the name of Berrigan put forward a rather different view of the business. Mental deficiency – if such was the root of the lad's behaviour and that remained to be proved – need be no drawback at all in a hired man. Hadn't his own first cousin, Murty Berrigan there beyond in Bawnmore, a half-eejit working for him for the best part of twenty years and there wasn't the equal of him anywhere in the length and breadth of Ireland for work? The Pooka* (as the man in question was nicknamed because of his preference for his own company) didn't give a divil's damn about wages, the rate collector announced, so long as he had a full pipe of tobacco and enough to eat.

"That was a different state of affairs altogether," Lar Buggy objected. "The Pooka mightn't be the full shilling but nobody ever heard him talking to himself in the middle of a field, so they didn't!"

"Well, sure, there's no harm in talking if that's all he does," Fintan Bolger maintained philosophically and there the matter rested. It would be too much to expect that these un-

*Púca in Irish; a hobgoblin or spirit, often malevolent.

16

imaginative gentlemen would have any inkling at all of the poetic urge that inspired Schnitzer's little foibles but in any case Fintan Bolger was not so foolish as to dispense with the poet's services. Why should he when the lad was an excellent worker, a model of industry, and content with a miserable wage?

Chapter Two

A PHOTOGRAPH OF Schnitzer O'Shea taken in or about his seventeenth year shows a raw-looking country youth with spiky, slicked-down hair and guileless eyes. A cheap tie-pin fastens the collar of his shirt and a Pioneer* pin reposes innocently side-by-side with a Guinness badge on the lapel of his jacket from the button-hole of which a watch-chain extends to his breast pocket: a bit of a sham, this, for it is well known that the lad did not possess a timepiece at this stage of his career! A cigarette hangs from the corner of the young man's mouth in imitation, no doubt, of the screen tough guys whose adventures he follows so keenly, and the scowl on his face is equally affected for according to general agreement it was greatly at variance with his genial and gentle nature.

Schnitzer had by now begun to write poetry which he sent in almost weekly to one or the other of the two newspapers earlier referred to, and even though the best of these compositions gave no promise at all of the stature he was to achieve in the years to come they brought him some recognition throughout the district. One such poem (if it may be dignified by the title) is still to be heard from time to time in the barony, set to a popular ballad air:

Farewell to sweet Muldowneyscourt, likewise to Mullaghbawn,
    farewell to lofty Tullabrin and sheltered, green Dromawn**
Farewell to Ballyhackett, Ballymack and Ballykeefe, and to think
    of dear old Skeoughvostheen fills my poor heart with grief.

Nothing of much value here, it will be agreed, but then perhaps even greater poets than O'Shea are ashamed of their earlier efforts – who knows what mediocrity even the Bard of Avon himself may have been guilty of while still a lad?

What is important is that Schnitzer was now absorbing all

---

*Total abstinence (from liquor). The Temperance Movement, contrary to outside belief, is very strong in Ireland.
**Properly Dromán an Iarainn. The origin is obscure but it is not, as is sometimes supposed, the iron ridge or mound. This would be Dromainn an Iarainn.

the feel and essence of Irish country life that would bloom so freshly in *Milestones,* his first collection of verse. A tireless cyclist he would, at the end of a long day's toil in the fields, fasten a pair of clips to the legs of his trousers, clap his cap back to front on his head and with a jubilant yell leap on his bike to set off for a long, punishing ride through the summer country-side. Schnitzer was a familiar sight as he hurtled along the dusty country bohareens, furiously pushing the old army bike with its heavy carbide lamp fixed in front, straining the muscles of his sturdy legs to exact the greatest speed from his creaking mount while he rapturously mouthed some succulent verbal tit-bit. *Caramba!* it might be, or *Sacre Bleu!* or even the more prosaic *Blimey!* Occasionally he would emit a high-pitched cry or scream a pet word at the hedges flying past – *Nidifugous!* it might be, or *Merovingian!* – and then, crouched over the handlebars he would skim like a swallow through the gathering dusk. One pictures him careering down some steep incline, exhilirated by the rush of wind buffeting his suntanned face or toiling manfully uphill, scorning to dismount however sharp the ascent until, reaching the summit, he surveys the rich Leinster pastures below. It was on such an occasion, very likely, that he composed "Farewell to Sweet Muldowneyscourt", committing the simple lines to memory first, in the manner of the old Irish bards, and writing them down later . . .

But there was a practical side to the poet's nature, too, and this was well demonstrated in the care and attention he lavished on his bike. Schnitzer was forever cleaning and repairing the machine, making little improvements and inno-vations of his own, scanning the tyres for sign of wear or inspecting the rims for a trace of rust; he never left it out overnight and each moving part was oiled to repletion. The policy of planned obsolescence had not yet reached Glenbeg but even Fintan Bolger was moved to comment that if everyone took such care of his property industrial production would cease altogether before long! Such was the poet's careful nature however. And not content with simply looking after his bicycle he also embellished it in various ways, affixing a little tricolour pennant to the front mudguard, for example, and sticking a profusion of little coloured transfers to the frame. The cumbersome old army bike was Schnitzer's Pegasus, the magic steed on which he fled the scenes of his daily toil, and there wasn't a townland in the barony of Glenbeg, nor perhaps in the whole of the County Kilkenny, that he did not pass through at some time. Once he even cycled to Tramore to get his first view of the sea, returning home again that evening: a round trip of ninety miles on a bike with only one gear! There is no doubt that Schnitzer's old bike can be seen as an extension of himself and the adornments he chose for it a form of self-expression: the raucous motor horn that served as a bell, the piece of cardboard attached to the rear fork to produce a whirring noise as it brushed the spokes, not to mention the spokes themselves painted in an array of bright colours that merged like a spinning roulette when he flashed by. Certainly his bicycle formed a large part of O'Shea's recreation, helping to consume whatever energy he had left after his day's work; and boredom, the bane of the youth of today, was something quite unknown to him.

A S A farm-labourer earning a mere pittance and, it must be said, a young man of uncertain pedigree, Schnitzer could hardly hope to find himself a sweetheart in a community the likes of which he grew up in. Men whose antecedents were better established than Schnitzer's often went through life as reluctant bachelors because of the inadequacy of their means: in a society that judges men by what they have rather than by what they are, personal worth is not always prized as it should be and the poet would need to have had the face and the form of Adonis to make up for his other disadvantages.

Schnitzer, of course, was no less susceptible to the charms of the opposite sex than any other young man and in the summer months he often attended the open-air dances, or danceboards as they were called, that were held on Sunday evenings in Ballybrack or Threecastles. Buxom country girls flocked to these events and it was only natural that Schnitzer should fall for one of them when he had often been smitten by the less substantial beauties who graced the cinema screen. As it happened he was singularly unwise in his choice of a real inamorata ... The cinema might well have presented O'Shea with the chance of meeting a young woman, a housemaid or laundry worker, perhaps, who would not have rejected him,

21

but if such opportunity ever offered itself he must have let it pass. Nor is there any suggestion in the poems that chronicle this period of his life that he was even awake to such likelihood: "The Latch of Wonder"* catches admirably that magical moment before the screen comes to life, the hushed expectancy when the lights dim, but there is no word at all of an assignation, of the romantic possibilities which the occasion might afford: and the picture-house was, after all, the trysting place of young folk in those days!

It was to Ned Purcell's daughter, Anastasia, that Schnitzer O'Shea gave his heart; unfortunately, since her status as a comfortable farmer's daughter placed her hopelessly beyond his reach. Of course if Schnitzer had been more aware of the social distinctions, the rigidly hierarchical nature of the community he lived in, this would have been only too clear to him. But poets are often blind to the petty realities of life and Schnitzer saw the object of his affection as a person without regard to the position she occupied in the material scheme of things. It must be admitted, also, that he did not know Miss Purcell very well, in truth scarcely at all though he sometimes partnered her for an old-time waltz or a Cashel set at the danceboards and he cycled a few hundred yards of the road with her one evening on his way through Skeoughmore. Although the young woman is not mentioned by name there is a long poem by Schnitzer in an old issue of the *Kilkenny People* which commemorates the event; it is an unremarkable com-

*This poem is included in Milestones, *his first volume of verse:*
Fourpence lifts
the latch of
wonder . . .
(Womb-dark, tomb-dark hall.)
Someone coughs, feet
shuffle.
The lights dim
and hearts lighten.

It is impossible to capture the racy economy of the Irish original in translation but we see how O'Shea makes use of contrasting images to good effect. Commenting on this Vidor T. Whitmere in his Poet in Hobnails *speaks of "a felicity of expression, illuminating as it is apt". Whitmere's study of the Glenbeg poet is, of course, immeasurably more perceptive than that of the American Walbark.*

position, to say the least, and perhaps two lines will suffice: "Our feelings tallied, we briefly dallied, my courage rallied along the way, That pleasant meeting was all too fleeting, our hearts were beating in vain that day."

Schnitzer was almost certainly mistaken in imagining that his feelings were shared by Anastasia Purcell and it is interesting to contrast an incomparably finer poem in Irish, "Danceboard Days" (*Milestones* p.13) with the vapidity of the lines just quoted:

Sturdy lads and lasses comely
fair of face and light of foot,
weaving, swinging, twirling blithely
till the tardy sun had set.

That Anastasia Purcell attended the danceboards at all is surprising for the daughters of the better-off farmers generally did not do so and in any case there would have been little opportunity for Schnitzer to develop the acquaintance; any undue attention on his part to the girl would have been noted with gleeful interest and be carried back in due course to Big Ned Purcell; a formidable individual to say the least. Thus Schnitzer could only worship from afar and voice the pain of unrequited love as follows:

The *sliotar** of love my grasp eluded
the whistle blew, the game concluded
and Purcell's daughter, the fairest far
shone far, remote, like an evening star.

It is no unkindness to Anastasia Purcell to say that she was not quite the raving beauty that Schnitzer perceived her to be. Either way, it is inconceivable that she would have accepted a proposal of marriage from the poet even if she had been allowed any say at all in the matter and not been subject to such firm (not to say despotic) parental control. As it was she can have had little inkling of the feelings entertained towards her by Fintan Bolger's servant boy, far less that he would have the temerity to ask her father if he might pay her court. Big Ned was a man unburdened by any feelings of refinement or

*Coming from a great hurling county it is not surprising that O'Shea should use the simile of a hurley ball. But again the inadequacy of translation does no justice to the original: the recurrence of "far" in the fourth line of the quatrain is an attempt to match the intricacies of the Gaelic internal rhyme. "Purcell's daughter" conveys affection in the original.

23

sensitivity, an arrogant, purse-proud farmer who reckoned everything in terms of cost and profit. He was, furthermore, given to ungovernable outbursts of temper, outbursts of such ferocity that none but the bravest or most foolhardy of men thought of offending him. "As awkward as Purcell" is a colloquialism still heard in Glenbeg and stories are told (some of them exaggerated no doubt) of the excesses of Big Ned when the tantrums seized him. Schnitzer O'Shea may have been as plucky as any young man in the district but approaching Ned Purcell as he did is surely more evidence of his honourable nature than of his physical courage, for he would hardly have gone near the Purcell place if he had any idea at all of the danger involved.

Schnitzer burned with love for Anastasia Purcell, she possessed his thoughts by night and day and the presumption of his love became a fillip to mischievous gossip; ludicrous rumours were manufactured and circulated and the matter provided conversation for many a company.

"Say, gents," Fintan Bolger announced to his friends in Podge Maher's one night, "that boy of mine is after falling in love, so he is!"

The comment did not arouse much interest, but then Fintan Bolger added: "He has a great notion of Ned Purcell's girl beyond in Skeoughmore!"

"Be the Holy Man!" said Lar Buggy aghast.

"I knew he wasn't right," said 'Más Delaney. "Begor, Big Ned'll take tay* wid him if he gets wind of it!"

"Be the living God he'll make 'brish' of him," Lar Buggy said solemnly.

"He'd slaughter a man for less, sure," opined 'Más Delaney.

But Podge Maher who was suspected of harbouring alien and anti-social ideas not in keeping with his place in the community took a different view. "Oh begor, Big Ned could pull aisy then; the lad could be good enough for his daughter, so he could! Ain't it in the Bible even, that the first shall be last and the last shall be first, and he that humbleth himself shall be exalted?"

"Begor now, Podge, saving your presence, that's as clear a

*An old Kilkenny colloquialism; it means to challenge, or accept a challenge, to fight.

24

case as ever I heard of the divil quoting scripture for his own ends," 'Más Delaney replied with asperity. "You're not going to tell me that O'Shea is as good as the big fella's daughter?"

"I thought we were all supposed to be the same in the sight of God," Podge Maher countered, but his customers would have none of it.

"We're not all the same in the eyes of Ned Purcell," 'Más Delaney reminded him, "and 'tis him that O'Shea will have to deal with if he hears of him looking at his daughter."

"He must be a woeful eejit altogether," marvelled Lar Buggy, and then they went on to other things.

They would have had greater cause for discussion, however, had they been present when Schnitzer called on Big Ned. Schnitzer's infatuation with Anastasia had been steadily growing, he breathed her name a million times a day as he raked the fragrant hay or thinned the drills of sugar-beet with practiced hands, and he traced her initials lovingly on every scrap of paper that came his way. *AP* he would inscribe with reverence, ornately interweaving the letters with tortuous Celtic designs, intricately convoluted ribbons that sprouted odd symbols at either end, and gaze on his handiwork as one bewitched. Verses of nine lines with the first letter in each line spelling *Anastasia* when read vertically he threw off with the speed of a bookie marking betting slips and sometimes, more ambitiously, he varied the form by setting out the nine letters in diagonal progression from beginning to end. Youth is entitled to its measure of sweet folly and it would be unfair to reproduce those gauche efforts here although they could hardly detract from the stature which he later achieved. And so the initial-writing and the versifying went on and the poet's obsession with Miss Purcell grew until one day, unable to bear the intensity of his yearning any longer, he forsook his labours, changed into his Sunday suit, plastered down his spiky hair with Brilliantine, jumped on his old army bike and set off at a frantic pace for Ned Purcell's farm in Skeoughmore. Where, without any preliminaries at all, he asked Big Ned if he might have the honour of courting his daughter.

One can only marvel here at Schnitzer's innocence and lack of worldly wisdom and it must be surmised that it was the influence of the innumerable American films he had seen

25

which prompted so reckless a course of action. For with the impressionability of youth O'Shea probably imagined he was following a well-defined procedure; he may have seen himself as some clean-cut Yankee teenager manfully asking permission to date the girl of his dreams. But of course things were ordered a little differently in Glenbeg and in any event Big Ned Purcell was not the kind of man to make allowance for whatever misapprehension Schnitzer may have been under. Big Ned, as already indicated, was prone to bouts of sudden and spiteful anger and only a little earlier that same day he had been provoked to an orgy of destruction.

It happened that Big Ned was leading a skittish cob through the haggard when a hen flew across their path, startling the cob and causing it to rear violently. Big Ned, instead of calming the horse as any rational man would do, directed his attention towards the hen, pursuing the unfortunate bird all over the haggard with threats and imprecations out of all proportion to the inconvenience it had caused. Squawking piteously the terrified fowl sought to elude him, until finally in a state of blind panic and near to collapse it flew into the farmhouse kitchen, alarming the cat and exciting the dog that had been asleep by the fire. Common prudence would have counselled withdrawal in order that the witless hen might emerge without creating too much havoc, but Ned Purcell was beyond the restraints of prudence now and what he did was to follow the hapless bird into the kitchen, seeking to grab it in his great, calloused hands. Bellowing like a maniac he lunged again and again at the terrified fowl, and again and again it evaded him, flying hither and thither in a manner never intended by nature in its frenetic bid to escape. As the hen fluttered against the dresser sending plates and vessels, some of Mrs Purcell's most prized possessions, crashing to the floor, the distraught woman begged Big Ned to desist before he and the hen had wrecked the kitchen between them; but he ignored her pleas and would gladly have laid his home in ruins, one feels, for the satisfaction of taking the wretched bird's life; a satisfaction to be denied him. For as he grabbed once more at the demented fowl it fell dead at his feet from a surfeit of terror, leaving the farmer clasping a fistful of feathers as he mouthed the foulest of blasphemies.

It will be agreed that Schnitzer could not have picked a less auspicious time for what was in any case a hopeless mission and his arrival at the Purcell place so soon after the little episode described could only arouse Big Ned to greater fury. It was the hired man on the Purcell farm, a raggedy fellow up from Slieverue, who witnessed the whole affair and apart from the man's weakness for drink – which must account to some extent for his scarecrow appearance – Tim Costigan is considered to be an honest and reliable source. Big Ned, it seems, was forking dung into a cart drawn by the cob that had taken fright earlier, when Schnitzer swung into the haggard on his bike, breathless with urgency and blithely unaware that he was treading on dangerous ground. Dismounting at a leap, Schnitzer threw his bicycle against the corner of the hayrick and with no more ado blurted out the reason for his visit. The farmer stared blankly at O'Shea for a moment and the look that spread over his face was terrible to behold, a black, malevolent look beside which the fabled basilisk's stare was a winsome smile; yet when Big Ned spoke it was with a calm that was even more menacing in its falsity.

"Excuse me, sonny, I don't think I heard you rightly. Would you mind saying that all over again?" he asked, and guilessly poor Schnitzer complied.

"I'd like to keep company with your daughter Anastasia, Mr Purcell. I'm asking for your permission to pay my respects." There was a dreadful silence before Ned Purcell spoke again.

"Be the Holy Man above but that's what I thought you said alright," he said softly, aghast at the shameless effrontery, the sheer cheek of Fintan Bolger's servant boy. He stared at Schnitzer as he might at some totally new form of life, some specimen of biped he had never seen before, and O'Shea, misconstruing the scrutiny, hastened to assure Big Ned that his intentions were entirely honourable and that it was with an ultimate view to marriage that he sought permission to call on Anastasia. It was at this juncture that Ned Purcell uttered a strange, inarticulate cry, a howl of anguish like that of a man who inadvertently dips his hand in a cauldron of boiling tar, and then, with the speed of a striking serpent, he lunged at the poet with his two-pronged fork – a vicious swipe that came within an ace of disembowelling O'Shea. The quickness of the young poet's reflexes saved him; but Big Ned brought the fork round again in a savage thrust that missed its target by the leanest of margins. Again Schnitzer leapt clear, imploring the farmer to hear him out, and again Big Ned sought to transfix him with the gleaming points of his fork while at the same time he poured a torrent of invective on the unfortunate youth, cataloguing the poverty of his maternal ancestry and speculating in the foulest way on the breed of his paternal forebears. What an infernal cheek, frothed Big Ned, as he wielded his pitchfork in great, slashing arcs from which Schnitzer retreated nimbly, what a damnable cheek from a pauper – of a long line of paupers – who owned nothing but the duds he stood up in! When the only bit of livestock that anyone belonging to him ever possessed was a couple of goats hobbling about on the long acre or nibbling a blade of grass at the bottom of the garden! What was the world coming to at all at all, Big Ned beseeched, when a penniless little whipper-snapper of a hired boy could insult a respectable man and his family? Or was there a God above anymore?

"Go 'long, you cur you, before I spill your puddins all over the haggard, you odious yoke you!" Big Ned foamed, striking again and again with his pitchfork in a manner that discouraged further attempt at parley. And by now, of course, Schnitzer was convinced of the futility of his suit, indeed his very life was at risk while he tarried on Purcell ground. The poet was not lacking in courage but neither was he totally bereft of discretion and so, recognising that he had nothing to gain from seeking to reason with Big Ned, he sprang on his trusty bike and shot away with a whirring of coloured spokes, followed by a cataract of abuse. This hostile reception may not have cooled Schnitzer's ardour for Ned Purcell's daughter but it certainly deterred him from ever approaching her father again.

A week later Schnitzer Theophilus O'Shea, poet in the making, was aboard the creaking old *Princess Maude* with his few belongings in a battered suitcase. His thoughts, we may be sure, were appropriate to the poignancy of the occasion, as he gazed sadly back at the purpling Wicklow hills and sighed for Anastasia Purcell, his first and only love.

28

❦❦❦ Chapter Three. ❦❦❦

SCHNITZER'S DESTINATION HAD been London and not the pleasant county town of Northmanton that is so often linked with his name. The poet would have been familiar with the names of the bigger towns and cities of Britain but it is doubtful if he ever heard more than a passing reference to Northmanton until the night before he first set foot there. Schnitzer's one-way ticket was to London and it was while still less than half-way across the Irish Sea that he was prevailed upon to go to Northmanton. The miscreants responsible for this change of itinerary were compatriots of his own. Every race and nation has its share of bad eggs no doubt, but it was unfortunate for O'Shea that he became involved with them at all.

Schnitzer remained on deck while Ireland was still in sight and indeed for some time after, gazing pensively into the thickening dusk and wondering what the future held for him in Britain. An earnest young lady, a voluntary worker from the Legion of Mary, talked to him for some time about the pitfalls which awaited the unwary and the innocent in England, urging him to remain true to the practice of his religion and by good example to uphold the honour of his native land. She pressed some prayer-leaflets on him and gave him a list of suitable addresses in London where he would find lodgings in good Catholic homes, and after she had moved on to speak to other travellers Schnitzer went below to the bar where he called for a glass of lemonade. This was a reasonable enough choice of drink for a young man of eighteen, one might think, but it attracted the notice of a trio of Connachtmen, navvies or seasonal labourers perhaps, who even at this early stage of the journey were well advanced towards intoxication. For some odd reason (there is no accounting for the vagaries of the drink-befuddled mind) Schnitzer's preference for lemonade reduced the three Connachtmen to a condition of helpless laughter. They slapped each other heartily and mimicked his request as though it were the funniest thing they had ever heard, and they

29

parrotted it over and over again to one another, howling all the while with laughter.

"Lemonade, on me sowkins!" bawled one of the trio, spilling Guinness down the front of his shirt.

"On me solemn oath; bleddy lemonade!" yelped another in hysterics.

"I own to Christ; *lemonade!*" shrieked the third before collapsing in a heap on the floor where he lay twitching with laughter.

It is to O'Shea's credit that he retained his dignity and ignored this loutish behaviour. In fact he was withdrawing from the crowded bar when one of the Connachtmen, fearing to be deprived of his fun, detained him.

"Sit down, ladeen*, sit down here along with us, sure we're only havin' a bit of the crack!" he entreated, at the same time pulling a chair rudely from another traveller who was about to occupy it.

"Sit down, awock**, sure we're only coddin'!" begged the second, while the third man, struggling to arise from the floor, was overcome by a fresh paroxysm of laughter and could not add to the invitation. Reluctant to appear uncivil and unsure how to respond to these uncouth fellows so different to the voyagers he saw acting so gentlemanly on the screen, Schnitzer did as he was bid and immediately the unlovely trio began to ply him with questions: what part of Ireland did he hail from, what was his occupation in life and what part of England was he bound for? Civil as ever Schnitzer told them that he hailed from the townland of Muldowneyscourt in the barony of Glenbeg and that he had spent the past few years working for Fintan Bolger in Dromawn Aneerin, and this very ordinary piece of intelligence provoked a fresh outburst of mirth.

"Muldowneys-Court, be the hokey! Muldowneys-Court, you say? Is it a big place, sonny?" asked one, pulling a face for the benefit of his companions.

"Arrah, why wouldn't it?" asked the second, pulling another face. "It's as big as Ballina, I'll bet!"

"As big as Belfast more likely," hazarded the third man,

*The diminutive form of "lad"; the word has connotations of affection or contempt, as applied.
**Irish A mhac, my son. The vocative case of mac which of course means "son".

getting up off the floor.

They questioned Schnitzer further; on the size and valuation of the Bolger farm in Dromawn Aneerin, on his wages and working conditions there, and on other matters related and unrelated; and every answer that Schnitzer gave, however politely or honestly, met with fresh guffaws of laughter. They asked him where he was bound for, pretending not to remember that he had already told them, and when he repeated that he was going to London they looked at each other as though they could scarcely believe their ears.

"Is it *London*, sonny? What in the name of God is bringing you to London?" one of them enquired much as he might ask what would bring anyone to Little Poddington or to some such obscure hamlet in the heart of rural England.

The trio shook their heads in sad disapproval, looking at Schnitzer as they would some valued friend whom they must protect from his own folly.

"London's played out, chap; there is nothing there anymore," said the first man.

"Not a light, kiddo!" affirmed the next.

"Not a bleddy sausage!" the third man said ruefully.

"London is bunched, awock! You might as well look for work on Achill Island!"

"At the top of Nephin!"

"In the town of Kiltimagh!"

"Or behind in Mulranny!"

These and other improbable locations were cited as examples of the scarcity of jobs in the English metropolis and not surprisingly Schnitzer protested: but the trio insisted that he was mistaken, that his information was now out of date.

"Sure all the work in London is done, now!"

"All the big buildings are built!"

"All the new gas mains are laid!"

"All the electric cable, too!"

"'Tis getting out of London the people are these days, ladeen."

"Anyone that has any go at all in him."

"Or not lying on the broad of his back in the hospital!"

"Or too old to stir."

"Or six feet under!"

This last piece of nonsense was the signal for a fresh burst of merriment and not unnaturally O'Shea was disturbed to have his high hopes so cruelly dashed. With his open and trusting nature it did not occur to him that the Connachtmen themselves were bound for London, a fact that could be ascertained from a glance at the amply labelled luggage lying at their feet. And then in a mood of further perfidy the three Connachtmen began discussing where best Schnitzer should go to secure worthwhile employment, employment that would bring him the kind of remuneration to which they felt sure his abilities entitled him. The better-known centres of industry like Manchester, Birmingham, Coventry and Sheffield were in turn examined and dismissed, and then, as though suddenly inspired, one of the men snapped his fingers and uttered a single word.

"Northmanton!"

This may well have been the first time that Schnitzer O'Shea ever heard of the town of Northmanton but the effect of the name on the two other men was to set them off into fits of laughter.

"Northmanton!" barked one of them. "Can we ever forget it?"

"Never in a million years!" shrieked his neighbour, jellified with mirth. "The best bleddy town in England for work!"

"Arrah, what England: in the whole of Great Britain!"

"In Europe," sobbed the third chap, his fist in his mouth.

"The whole flamin' world!" gasped the first man, clutching his heaving sides.

It seems odd that after this exhibition of buffoonery the unscrupulous trio should manage to persuade Schnitzer to abandon the idea of going to London and to get off the *Irish Mail* at the ungodly hour of four o'clock in the morning in Rugby midland station and there wait for three hours, almost, for a train on the branch line to Northmanton, some twenty or so miles away. But persuade him they did and thus it was that in the cold grey chill of an English dawn the young man from Glenbeg found himself on the draughty platform in Northmanton dazed and bewildered by a multiplicity of new impressions, the unintelligible English accents all about him, the noise and bustle so far removed from the quiet of Dromawn Aneerin. It is not hard to imagine how daunted the young country lad must have been by these alien surroundings, how

32

he must have momentarily longed for the familiarity of Dromawn Aneerin, the security of his old employment. However, he thrust these yearnings from him manfully and addressed himself to the realities at hand, mindful of the advice that Fintan Bolger had given him only the day before when they parted in Kilkenny.

"There's two things a man needs in a strange country," Fintan Bolger told Schnitzer as he pressed the gift of a ten shilling note into his hand. "The two things that a man needs in a strange country are work and lodgings. For you see sonny, if a man has work he can pay for his lodgings and if he has lodgings he can go to his work!"

Schnitzer did not question the validity of this, but now as he stood among the scurrying workers either boarding trains for somewhere else or pouring out of the train that had brought him from Rugby he wondered how to go about implementing the farmer's advice. The scene of early morning activity must have struck the young poet as particularly strange, causing him to wonder, maybe, if the good people of England went to bed at all. And no doubt the inexplicable good humour of the workers at so early an hour, the cheery "Oi! Oi!" and "Good morning!" they called to one another, struck him as odder still. Such little niceties were not common in rural Ireland where unnecessary chatter first thing in the morning would have been coolly received. Schnitzer may have wondered like many another exile from the quiet land of Erin if he could ever adapt to this hectic way of living at all and if he had not made a mistake in leaving Glenbeg; but God's help, to quote the old Irish proverb, is nearer than the door and it came to Schnitzer in the shape of a burly railway porter whose facial characteristics declared him a Hibernian as unmistakably as if he had proclaimed it in his broad Tipperary accent.

The porter was pulling a handcart laden with newsprint but he halted when his eyes fell on O'Shea and then, with the familiarity of one Irishman greeting another when they are far from home, he asked if Schnitzer had just come over. Delighted to hear a recognisable accent Schnitzer confirmed that this was so, adding that his intention had been to go to London but that some fellows he met on the boat had told him that there were much better work-prospects in Northmanton, that in truth there was no town to equal Northmanton for work and wages in the length and breadth of Britain. The porter heard this with an appropriate look of surprise for it was far removed from the truth: Northmanton had as yet escaped the mania for expansion and development that had disfigured so many English towns and consequently the type of employment which the three jokers had in mind was less plentiful there than in other areas. The Connachtmen knew this from experience, of course, and that was why they had misdirected Schnitzer.

"I wonder would you be able to tell me where I'd get work and lodgings?" Schnitzer asked the porter and added Fintan Bolger's maxim to underline his earnestness. But the Tipperary porter seemed to be more concerned with the lack of employment in Ireland – or to be more precise, with the historical reasons for it – than with the question Schnitzer had put to him, and with no more ado he launched into a bitter tirade against the evils of British rule in Ireland, how Ireland's once-flourishing industries had been killed off by the London parliament.

"You know what they done to the linen industry in Belfast, don't you?" he challenged O'Shea; and before Schnitzer could admit that he had no idea at all what they had done to the linen industry in Belfast the porter went on: "Of course you do boy, you know your history, you learned it at school like us all! They crippled the Belfast linen trade with their high tariffs so that it couldn't compete with their own! And the same with the wool trade! You read *Jail Journal*, boy, you know what John Mitchell said about the wool merchants of Bradford, how they strangled our thriving woollen industry back in the sixteenth century! And sure what about our oak woods, boy, you know what they done to our oak woods?"

Oak woods were not a very prominent feature of the Irish landscape to the best of Schnitzer's recollection nor, it must be admitted, did he know what it was that a malign English administration had done, or was alleged to have done, to such woods; history books had not been among the reading matter supplied to him by Mrs Bolger and he had not stayed long enough at school to learn much of the subject. It was no matter, for the Tipperaryman was intent on telling him, to the neglect of the duties he should have been performing.

"They cut them down, boy, didn't they? Sure you know that yourself, doesn't everyone? They cut down the lovely oak

34

forests that covered the face of Munster to build their bleddy
ships – Raleigh and Drake and Spenser the Poet and Good
Queen Bess and the rest of the pirate gang! They cut down our
beautiful oak woods to build ships so they could rob the poor
Spaniards of their gold! Sure you know the song, don't you,
"Cad a dhéinimid feasta gan adhmad?" *

Gratified to have an audience, albeit a captive one, the
porter chuntered on and on, sketching the many unhappy
episodes of Irish history from the landing of the Anglo-
Normans in 1169 through to the rapacity of Henry the
Eighthand Oliver Cromwell, to the Penal Laws that followed
the break-up of the old Gaelic system, to the ruthless
suppression of the rebellion of 1798; the Great Famine, the
Black and Tans and the machinations of the nefarious
Welshman, Lloyd George, in partitioning Ireland . . . In the
course of this lecture the porter threw dates at Schnitzer with
all the accuracy of a darts champion scoring bull's-eyes in a
tournament, and fixing the poet with an outraged glare he
demanded:

"You know all about 1691, don't you? And 1803? When
they hanged poor Emmet the darling of Erin? To be sure you
do, boy, doesn't the whole world know it? And about
Mullaghmast where they massacred our chieftains at the
banquet table?"

It was here that Schnitzer interrupted to remind the porter
that work and lodgings were his immediate concern, and
recalled to the present the Tipperaryman focused his gaze on
the poet as though becoming properly aware of him for the first
time.

"Lodgings, boy? Faith then I can, that's no problem at all,
sure! I can give you the address of a good Catholic house, so I
can, a house that observes the rule of abstinence on Friday,
not like a lot of them I could mention. Do you drink?"

Schnitzer assured the porter that apart from the occasional
glass of stout or Smithwick's Ale at the treshing he had hardly
ever tasted alcohol and the porter nodded approvingly.

"Good man yourself! Sure wasn't it drink that was the curse
of the Irish always? Wasn't it drink that beat the men of '98?

* *An old Gaelic lament for the oak woods of Munster denuded by the Elizabethans
to build the English fleet.*

35

Wasn't it drink that loosened the tongue of Rory O'Moore on the eve of the '41 Rebellion? Wasn't every traitor and turncoat we ever had a drunkard?"

Schnitzer hastened to reaffirm his disinterest in drink and begged his compatriot to confine himself to the matter in hand and, thus pressed, the porter wrote out an address for him, the house of a good-living Irishwoman who would see that he attended his religious duties, for Mrs O'Connor wouldn't have an infidel under her roof, not if he paid her a hundred pounds a week! As to the employment situation in Northmanton, well he would get a job right enough, no doubt, but not as easily as those gentlemen on the boat seemed to imagine. Most of the lads used the pub as a kind of labour exchange, the porter said, but Schnitzer would do better patronizing St Briget's Club (which was unlicensed for drink); he would meet other Irish boys and girls there and find out all about the prospects of work. Club, church and Delia O'Connor's lodging house were all within a dog's trot of each other and so a man need have no fear of being lonely, indeed you'd almost think you were somewhere in Ireland.

Eager to be off, Schnitzer thanked the Tipperary porter who gave him one last piece of advice. There was a newspaper called the *Irish Democrat* which was sold outside St Bridget's Club (though not within because Father Murphy wouldn't permit it!) and it generally carried a list of jobs in the building industry. If all fruits failed he might buy a copy of the *Democrat*, the porter suggested to Schnitzer, but he wouldn't recommend it as reading material for it was a communist rag as everyone knew, and financed by the Kremlin!*

Armed with this advice and information Schnitzer made his way uncertainly up through the streets of Northmanton, marvelling at the volume of the morning traffic and the number of shops already open and doing business; in Kilkenny, let alone Muldowneyscourt, there would be very little commercial activity before ten o'clock! On his way Schnitzer was obliged to seek directions more than once but though he found the citizens of Northmanton helpful and courteous in the extreme their speech was so hard to follow as to be useless.

*The porter was repeating a canard widespread at the time; in fact there is no evidence at all that the Kremlin poured vast sums into the journal in question.

If it had been to the USA that Schnitzer had emigrated like the better-off members of the rural community he grew up in he would have had no difficulty in understanding all that was being said to him for of course his ear had become attuned to American speech in the cinema; indeed had he come across an Englishman who spoke the language of the BBC he would have had no great problem, either. But the Northmantonian variant of English with its deep vowels and its skimped consonants left him sorely puzzled. Eventually, however, he reached Balaclava Terrace, a crumbling row of once-stately Victorian villas now set off into flats and bedsitters with a number of overcrowded lodging houses in between.

Schnitzer O'Shea was not fated to stay with Mrs O'Connor, as happens, for on pressing her doorbell he was told regretfully that she must refuse him; she would gladly have taken him in, Delia O'Connor assured Schnitzer, even if it had meant putting a mattress on the floor for him, but some grudging old busybody had reported her to the authorities and in consequence of this un-neighbourly act a health inspector had been round to warn her of the penalties for overcrowding. The best she could do for him, Mrs O'Connor said, was to send him along a few doors to Mrs Perkins, an English lady who always had vacancies. Schnitzer thanked her and went along to the house, ravenously hungry now and a little tired after his long journey overnight. Again he pressed the doorbell and in a moment Mrs Perkins – or Mother Perkins as she liked her lodgers to call her – appeared, her eyes screwed up against the cigarette smoke from the Lucky Strike that adhered to her lip. An angular lady with spectacles permanently askew and an air of quiet help-lessness, Mother Perkins regarded the young man from Glenbeg with a perhaps pardonable look of suspicion; all too often Mother Perkins took in lodgers who proved a bad risk, unlike her neighbour Mrs O'Connor, an altogether more shrewd judge of humanity.

"Blest if I know, boy," Mother Perkins admitted as she surveyed the poet doubtfully. "I suppose I could put you in with Ginger, if that's all right with you."

The custom of bed-sharing, with two or even three lodgers occupying a double bed, was common enough at the time and it never gave rise to the kind of distasteful speculation that such an arrangement would provoke in the more "broad-minded" climate of today; Schnitzer, no sybarite, accepted the offer instantly.

"Best come in then," Mother Perkins said and Schnitzer followed her upstairs where she showed him the bed he would share with a compatriot of his own, a Donegalman named Ginger McGinn, a man of such unwavering devotion to Mammon that he happily worked seven days a week and would as happily have worked an eighth had the week been so constituted.

"Ginger's a grafter," Mother Perkins told the poet with approval. "Never misses a minute from work."

Downstairs in her basement dining-room Mother Perkins set a rather insubstantial breakfast of sliced bread and baked beans before Schnitzer who wolfed it down greedily as she prattled away to him over her tea cup, never dreaming that most of her conversation was lost on her new guest.

"Of course, I'm Irish too," Mother Perkins told Schnitzer as he cleaned his plate with the wafer-thin sliced loaf so different from the home-baked bread he had been used to in Dromawn Aneerin. "Oh yes, boy; dear Lord yes! Mother Perkins is as Irish as they come, as Irish as the dear old Blarney Stone!"

Though he was understandably sceptical of the claim Schnitzer did not contest it; he was too polite to do so, of course, and already he suspected that the tea cup which the landlady kept sipping at contained a rather more potent brew than his own. In time he would become used to the so flattering English tendency to claim Irish ancestry, however remote.

"Oh yes, boy, I'm Irish on my old grandfather's side – the dear Lord rest his soul – and that's why I look after you Irish boys so well, just like I was your own real mother. Straight up, mate!" she said with a hint of challenge. "Nobody runs down the Irish when Mother Perkins is about, not bleedin' likely!" She rapped her now empty cup with such force on the table that Schnitzer could no longer doubt that she was three sheets in the wind and for a moment the realisation unnerved him; up to now the only females he had seen under the influence of drink were the travelling women who had their own code of behaviour. It was a situation that left him at something of a loss but with commendable tact he thanked her for her solicitude and announced his intention of looking for work.

"Yes boy," the landlady said and offered him a pinch of mentholated snuff from the little box placed beside her on the table, "I daresay you'll find summat easy enough, t'aint like when I was a gal, bleedin' millions on the dole! People ain't so silly today, Pat, they'd never stand for that sort of thing again. You can say what you like about old Adolf but if it hadn't bin for him and his silly bleedin' capers we'd still have two million on the bleedin' dole!"

Schnitzer accepted the pinch of snuff but forebore to comment for he was not sure that he understood much of what his new landlady had said; indeed it would be some time yet before he learned to feel at ease with Lavinia Perkins, a quite remarkable woman.

✾✾✾ Chapter Four. ✾✾✾

AS HE WENT vainly that first day from building site to factory and from factory to warehouse Schnitzer began to fear that his landlady's optimism was misplaced; he drew a blank in these and the many other places he tried. That evening, after he had eaten the insufficient dinner which the inebriated Mother Perkins put before him, he set off for St Bridget's Club as the railway porter had advised him to do. St Bridget's was a cheerless wartime structure adjacent to the old brownstone church of St Botolph, but what it lacked in amenities or comfort it made up in the conviviality of the members who gathered there nightly under the Papal flag and the Irish tricolour to read the *Catholic Herald* or the *Irish Press* (the only two papers that Fr Murphy, the club chairman, tolerated) and to talk about home. Schnitzer was not unaware that his countrymen and women were flocking to Britain in great numbers but he was genuinely amazed to find so many of them before him here in Northmanton. St Bridget's catered for a score or more on even the quietest nights and at the weekend when a dance was held there it was thronged to the door; the pubs round the area were well patronized by the Irish, and all of the building sites that Schnitzer had visited that day seemed to have their share of them too. More surprisingly still there was a deal of Irish spoken by some of these expatriates. In fact Schnitzer would hear more of his native tongue spoken in one week in Northmanton than he had ever heard at home in Glenbeg; apart, of course, from his grandfather who in his latter years spoke nothing else.

As a newcomer Schnitzer was welcomed to St Bridget's by Fr Murphy; the club, Fr Murphy impressed on him, was a haven, a little oasis in a desert of Godlessness, a beacon whose light helped dispel the curious notions which the indigent population tended to harbour about the Irish; he hoped that Schnitzer would find in St Bridget's an antidote to that loneliness which must always be the lot of the exile. Too many Irishmen, Fr Murphy lamented with darkening brow, sought comfort in the public bars of the town, squandering hard-

41

earned money that could be used to better purpose. The Church had a growing membership in many parts of Britain now and more churches would have to be built to accommodate the increase; instead of enriching the breweries and earning themselves a reputation for drunkenness, a lot of Irishmen would be better employed giving a few extra shillings to the Church. Fr Murphy left Schnitzer to mull over these words but the poet was more urgently concerned with the business of getting a job, and to be fair to his compatriots they were only too eager to help. A Kerry girl, still proudly attired in her blue clippie's uniform and leather cash-bag, told him he might get on as a conductor if he called to the bus depot at William's End and a Rathdowney man who worked in a shoe factory gave him a note to take to a foreman there; a Leitrim carpenter promised to ask for him on the site where he himself worked and a pipelayer with the firm of McAlpine said he'd try to get him the start as a labourer.

As happened, however, Schnitzer found other and even more lucrative employment. That night, as he made his way back to his lodgings in Balaclava Terrace, he ran into yet another Irishman, a down-at-heel fellow who asked for a cigarette, and as they smoked a Woodbine companionably together the man told Schnitzer that he should look for work in a navvy gang where no skill beyond the ability to wield a pick and shovel would be needed and the wages were three pounds a day. Accustomed all his life to modest remuneration O'Shea could hardly believe that any employer would be capable of such generosity: but generosity did not come into it, his informant explained, and the Mule Kennedy (the gentleman in charge of the cable-laying gang) would expect him to earn the money twice over. Still, the very thought of three whole pounds a day was enough to make Schnitzer dizzy with anticipation and that night, while Ginger McGinn snored peacefully beside him, he lay awake for ages thinking of the riches he could earn as a navvy.

Next morning Schnitzer made his way as directed to the pick-up point outside a pub called the Navvy's Rest where the contractors' lorries stopped to take on their human cargo. It was not yet seven o'clock and the orange streetlight shed a billious glow on the group of tousled-haired, nail-booted labourers stamping their feet on the damp pavement and

42

lamenting the excesses of the night before when they blew their day's pay in the licensed premises outside which they were now gathered. * Nobody took any notice of Schnitzer for new starters were common enough in that kind of work (those unable to perform satisfactorily being summarily dismissed within a matter of hours) and when the lorry arrived the men scrambled aboard as eagerly as if they were going on a day's outing and not to a day's back-breaking toil. The Mule Kennedy (whose nickname suggested a certain perversity of nature) sat in front with the driver and Schnitzer approached him, tremulous with hope, to ask if there was any chance of a job. Schnitzer's diffidence was uncalled for, did he but know it, for Paddy Kennedy was a good judge of labouring men and he could see that the Muldowneyscourt man merited a trial at least.

"Jump on the waggon, fella, and we'll see what you're like!" he told the poet and, incoherent with gratitude, Schnitzer joined his new workmates on the back of the lorry. One of the men thumped the roof of the driver's cab with his fist as a signal that they were all aboard and the lorry drove off, Schnitzer delirious with joy at having landed such a well-paid job so soon and quite unaffected by the gruffness of the other men around him. Three pounds per day when he had not yet begun to get that much per week as a farm labourer in Dromawn Aneerin! It was all he could do to restrain himself from yelling out "Hippophagy!" a word he had recently found in an old encyclopedia he'd picked up for a few pence in Kilkenny and which, together with the dictionary Mary Ellen Bolger had given him, made up most of the contents of his suitcase the day he left home.

Schnitzer O'Shea was not unaccustomed to hard graft, to long working hours or to harsh conditions, but even he was taken aback by the unremmiting pace and the fury of effort that was asked of the Mule Kennedy's gang. The work was entirely manual and the men worked in pairs, each pair

*It was customary in this kind of employment to pay the men on a daily basis, a detrimental practice for the availability of money for a nightly binge and the necessity of earning the same again next day kept them on a treadmill that was hard to escape. Vide Sub Daily: The Recollections of a Tramp Navvy by Paddy Heggarty, The Workers Press.

excavating an alloted length of trench before moving on to the next stretch, the front man breaking the ground with savage thrusts of his heavy digging-fork while his companion shovelled out the soil with such frantic haste that one might imagine he was unearthing a hidden treasure. When a sufficient length of trench had been excavated the heavy electric cable would be hauled into place to a succession of exhortive "Hups!" from the Mule Kennedy and then the work of backfilling began with frenzied urgency. O'Shea had worked hard for Fintan Bolger, but not that hard, and his already-calloused hands had fresh blisters before the day was out. What bothered him more than the strenuous nature of navvying, however, was the agressiveness of the other members of the gang, their brusqueness and incivility to each other, the outbursts of bad language and foul temper which accompanied almost every task. There were times when the mild-mannered O'Shea longed for the blessed solitude of the fields he had worked in at home, where apart from such as Big Ned Purcell there were few exhibitions of rancour and where a man was free to whisper – to even shout – some cherished word or expression. To do so in the navvy gang would have been unthinkable, an invitation to ridicule; and so the poet learned to curb the temptation and to concentrate on his work, consoling himself with the thought of the munificence of his three pounds a day. Even so there were pitfalls: on his first day in the cable-laying gang Schnitzer paused to roll himself a cigarette, a thrifty practice dictated by circumstance up to now, but before he had completed this simple operation an enraged Mule Kennedy loomed above him: "I don't mind you smoking them, sonny, but if you want to manufacture them you'd better go and look for a job in a fag-factory!" he snarled, and thereafter Schnitzer made sure to have his daily supply of cigarettes rolled and ready before he left the digs each morning.

Oddly enough Schnitzer O'Shea was not very popular with his fellow-navvies although they were all compatriots of his with even a couple of Kilkennymen in their number. Schnitzer's ability to "horse it out"* was never in question or he would not have lasted beyond the first day; it was rather his unsociable nature (as the others saw it) that earned their

* A navvy expression, it means to dig manfully. Sometimes "dog it out".

dislike. The men worked in pairs as already stated and since most of them were disinclined to partner Schnitzer it generally fell to a youngster called Owenie Garrigan to work opposite the poet. Owenie Garrigan was an unremarkable young man whose natural taciturnity was enhanced by a severe stammer, so even if there had been much time for idle chatter it is unlikely that there would have been in the way of exchange.

The pub was where the events of the day were discussed, nightly, by the Mule Kennedy's gang for every evening when they came off the lorry outside the Navvy's Rest they repaired there – every man-jack with the exception of Schnitzer – to drink pints of light and bitter until closing time when in all charity their condition could hardly be called sober. Alone of all the gang Schnitzer went straight to his lodgings and to the dinner that awaited him. The Mule Kennedy himself drank with his men every night and he made no bones at all about calling O'Shea a bad mixer: if a man was good enough to work with he was good enough to drink with, the Mule reckoned, and it was "a quare man that wouldn't have a gargle with his muckers!" In the beginning there was a deal of pressure on the Glenbeg man to join the others in their nightly indulgence in the Navvy's Rest, and it is to his credit that he withstood it so well and so stoically endured the contempt which his abstemiousness earned him.

SCHNITZER HAD now come to what was probably the happiest period of his life. He was gainfully employed, earning more money than he could easily spend, while at the same time he could enjoy his leisure hours to the full. He still sighed for Anastasia Purcell, to be sure, but less often with the passage of time; and though far from his homeland he did not suffer the pangs of homesickness unduly: all of his workmates were Irish, as were most of his fellow lodgers, and he could always wander up to St Bridget's Club if he felt in need of a further breath of home. The club did not attract O'Shea greatly, however, and it was to the cinema that he went almost nightly, to the Tivoli or the Picturedrome or the Ritz or the Gaumont; the Cinema-de-Luxe, the Coliseum, the Regal, the Savoy, the Roxy or to the old red-bricked Temperance Hall. In those days Northmanton did not want for picture halls whatever other cultural amenities it may have lacked. The poet patronized and loved them all and he catalogued them fondly in his last and greatest work though he had by then outgrown the spell of the "womb-dark, tomb-dark hall".

If the feeding in Mother Perkins' house left a lot to be desired Schnitzer was not among those who complained for he could always have a supper of fish and chips on his way home from the pictures at night or buy a loaf of bread and a quarter of ham in the corner shop to see him through the day. Schnitzer was no great lover of comfort and so it was neither the poor fare which Lavinia Perkins put before him nor the necessity of sharing a bed with the snoring Donegalman that almost caused him to seek other accommodation when he had been only a few days in Balaclava Terrace; it was the landlady herself, or rather her drinking habits, that almost decided him to pack his belongings and go. Mother Perkins was sadly addicted to drink. Moreover, her toleration of alcohol was quite low so that even after a few bottles of milk stout and a chaser or two of gin her personality sometimes underwent a startling transformation, a metamorphosis that Schnitzer could not but compare with that of the wretched Dr Jekyll he had seen in the cinema. And for some reason Mother Perkins was particularly prone to these changes of demeanour on Sundays, on Sunday nights to be precise, when she returned from the Hope & Glory public house across the way. Lavinia Perkins was not a church-goer but she had religious leanings of a maudlin and dogmatic nature and before she set off for her local on Sunday evenings she would listen to "Songs of Praise" on the wireless, joining the hymn-singing in her quavering voice; much to the disgust of those of her lodgers who had perforce to listen, not having the money themselves to go to the boozer. The ending of the programme was the signal for Mother Perkins to don her old moth-eaten coat and sally forth to the pub, and she would excuse herself quite needlessly, pleading the need for some little relaxation after a long week of cleaning and cooking for them all; as though these trips were weekly and not twice-daily events that generally resulted in worse that usual dinners for her men.

The Hope & Glory was a favourite meeting place for the landladies of the area (all but Mrs O'Connor who believed that drink was a failing best left to the male sex) and there they

46

discussed matters relevant to their trade, the ruinous appetites of Irish labourers and the deplorable tendency of some of them to do a flit without paying their dues. But Lavinia was less than welcome at these little conferences because of her quarrelsome disposition in drink, and equally for her propensity for making unsettling remarks such as, "God sees all, you know: He ain't blind!" apropos of nothing at all. On many and many an occasion Mother Perkins had to be asked to leave the Hope & Glory when her comments upset customers or threatened to create a disturbance, but even when the evening passed without incident she was sure to return to Balaclava Terrace in such a reversal of mood as to completely unnerve the more timid among her lodgers and send them scurrying for fresh accommodation next day.

Schnitzer had been drifting off to sleep that first Sunday night when he was rudely aroused by Mother Perkins bellowing from the hallway below that she wanted all her lodgers out at once. The bellowing continued for a little while and then, finding herself unheeded, the landlady began advancing up the stairs, pausing every couple of steps or so to renew her demand; and finally she was standing outside Schnitzer's bedroom door, screaming shrilly that she wanted them all out at once.

"Are you lot deaf, or summat? I said *out*, mate, and I mean *out!* You shower of bleeders are finished making a convenience of Mother Perkins: the party's over, chaps! Out, I say, before I fetch the bleedin' Law!" At this stage some of the more uncouth among the lodgers began to abuse the landlady in turn, calling to her in the most ungentlemanly language to go to her bed and not be making a so-and-so spectacle of herself before the world; and this, not unnaturally, served only to infuriate the poor woman all the more.

"Am I talking to myself then, playmates? You've got five minutes to pack before I call in the rozzers! I've had it with you lot, you can all piss off back to Ireland. This house goes on the market tomorrow and then it's a nice little villa in the Isle of Wight for Lavinia. I'm damned if I'll spend another day slaving my guts out for you ungrateful lot of bleeders!"

We all have our little dreams to sustain us in life and the Isle of Wight had come to be a kind of Shangri-La in Mother Perkins' mind, a haven of peace where she could end her days untroubled by the many creditors who plagued her; but this was Schnitzer's first experience of her unladylike behaviour and, dismayed, he sat up in bed only to be assured by Ginger McGinn that there was no need for alarm, that this was just a vagary that struck the old dear when she had one or two over the top or when someone upset her across in the pub.

"Don't heed her at all, she'll be as right as rain in the morning," Ginger McGinn told his bedfellow, and so it proved. Indeed it must be said that far from intimidating the less sensitive among her guests these tantrums only provoked them to even greater rudeness which in turn egged Lavinia on to shriller abuse until, worn out by the contretemps, she retreated to her own room downstairs where she snuffed and scolded tearfully before sleep overcame her. Next morning Mother Perkins was her usual self and neither she nor any of her lodgers referred to the goings-on of the night before.

Schnitzer O'Shea spent over a year working happily in the Mule Kennedy's gang and he would have worked there for the rest of his life, no doubt, had the choice been his. But it wasn't, because one day when they had completed a long strip of trench, tucked the electric cable safely away in the ground and restored the ravaged surface of the footpath to a semblance of its former state, the Mule Kennedy called his men together to tell them that they were out of a job, a piece of bad news they received with an equanimity that shocked the young poet from Glenbeg. It all had to do with estimates, with greedy, undercutting rivals and with other matters that need not concern them, the Mule said; and so, if they would just sling their digging tools in the back of the waggon they could all return forthwith to Northmanton in time for a few jars in the Navvy's Rest before it closed for the afternoon.

Schnitzer was dismayed to find himself so suddenly unemployed and he was sorely puzzled at the readiness with which the other men leapt at their ganger's suggestion, the alacrity with which they threw their picks and shovels and heavy digging forks on the back of the lorry, scrambling over each other in their eagerness to be away. To Schnitzer it was a doleful occasion and not a reason for further celebration. Nor did he accompany the rest of the gang into the Navvy's Rest when the lorry drew up there an hour or so later. It was still only the middle of the day, an ordinary working day at that, and even if he had been a drinking man it would have been quite contrary to his instincts and upbringing to sit swilling ale at such an hour. The others took a dim view of Schnitzer's refusal to join them on this, their last working day together, regarding it as further proof of his curmudgeonly nature. He wasn't an Irishman at all, they sneered, forgetting that O'Shea was a far more worthy representative of his native land than they could ever hope to be.

"Feck off with yourself, so, and count your friggin' money," an unpleasant character called Foot-iron* Kelly told the poet; and O'Shea, preoccupied now with the need of finding another job, did not deign to reply.

By this time, of course, Schnitzer had the advantage of knowing Northmanton almost as well as if he had been born and bred there, due largely to his habit of taking long walks on Sunday afternoons when his fellow lodgers were sleeping-off their midday booze; there wasn't a building site or a civil engineering project within miles around that he couldn't have made his way to blindfold. Thus it was that even before the Mule Kennedy and his merry men had been turned out of the Navvy's Rest that afternoon, Schnitzer had found himself a job on a block of high-rise flats being built on the edge of the town.

---

* The nickname derives from the implement – a flat piece of metal worn under the sole of the boot and secured by leather thongs at the instep – which is designed to protect the leather from being cut by the rim of spade or shovel. See again Paddy Hegarty's Sub Daily for comments on this and other strange symbols of prestige then current among the muck-shifting fraternity. Chapter Six (Inverted Values: the Navvy as a food snob!) is of particular sociological interest: navvies tended to despise fish and chips and other such light meals and would hoot derisively at factory workers queued up outside the "chipper". Hegarty quotes also those well-known lines of doggerel, "I'm Pincher Brown from Camden Town/ I like my eggs and bacon/ If you think I'll eat your fish and chips/ You're bleddy well mistaken!" This was supposedly addressed to a landlady who served up fish and chips to the renowned Pincher Brown for dinner one day! A "Pincher" was a timberman who shored up deep trenches.

❧❧ Chapter Five. ❧❧

SCHNITZER WAS EVEN happier as a builder's labourer than he had been as a cable-navvy. The work was more varied and less arduous and there were benefits undreamt of in the Mule Kennedy's gang; an annual holiday scheme with pay, a canteen where they served hot meals and a drying room where wet clothing could be hung overnight. Admittedly the pay was not so good but the workers were more pleasant and nobody sought to inveigle the poet into drinking at the end of the day. The foremen and gangers in charge were more civil than the Mule Kennedy, rarely ever swearing at the labourers or threatening them with instant dismissal, as the Mule did, when some difference of opinion arose. The site had been "organised" by the Allied Building Union (ABU) from the very start and Consolidated Construction had no wish to provoke needless disputes. All in all Schnitzer thought it a wonderful place to work and he threw himself into every task with such joyous enthusiasm that before long he attracted the attention of management and union alike. If a delivery of several thousand bricks was being unloaded Schnitzer handled seven or eight to every other man's five or six, and where other men tended to trundle their barrows of concrete along O'Shea would break into a gallop with his. When a huge lorry-load of cement rumbled onto the job many of the labourers had a habit of disappearing from sight but Schnitzer would go forward to meet it, rejoicing in the strength that allowed him to toss the hundredweight sacks about as though they were packets of tea. And he was no less diligent than he was industrious for he was always among the first to clock-on in the morning and among the very last to clock-off at the end of the day.

Such conscientiousness did not go unacknowledged by Consolidated Construction and when a vacancy for a brick-layer's labourer occurred O'Shea was offered the job. As a brickie's labourer his wages would be greatly increased (he would, of course, have to work harder still) and this was enough to make him jump at the offer: a decision that was to have far-reaching, not to say incalculable effects on the poet's

51

life.

The job of bricklayer's labourer suited Schnitzer even better because now he worked alone most of the time, operating his own mortar mixer and carrying the bricks and mortar aloft to the two bricklayers he served on the scaffolding. It was a liberating experience to be working alone again, an opportunity to indulge his little weakness for words: the rasping of the mixer drum as he fed it sand and cement meant he could mouth the most outlandish expressions without fear of being heard, words he had mined lovingly from the tattered pages of his encyclopedia and dictionary, words of such rarity as "zaporogian" or maybe "voraginious". Yet again it might be some English or even Welsh placename that fired his imagination, Ashby-de-la-Zouch or Kingston Bagpuize, or Llanfairfeachan or Bettyscoed. *Bet-tys-co-ed*, he would intone, thrilling to the rhythmical sound of it and increasing its volume and tempo until it seemed to him and that he was hearing again the clacking wheels of the train that had brought him from Holyhead through the long, lonely night to his new life in Northmanton. *Bettyscoed!* he might scream when the roar of pneumatic drills drowned out every other sound, or murmur it softly as he tipped the creamy mortar from the mixer drum to have it go "plop!" like fresh cowdung on the sheet of plywood underneath. And if perchance he was ever caught out indulging himself in this manner the poet could always pretend to be singing, or even swearing, because of course very few of the words which he incanted were known to the other men on the site.

This mild eccentricity was part and parcel of O'Shea's creative process, each separate word holding as much value for him as the many verses he was composing all the while now, stringing fluent (if unremarkable) lines together as he set out the facing-bricks on the scaffolding or dumped the fluid mortar from his hod onto the spotboards placed at regular intervals about. The hard physical toil which he embraced with such fervour stimulated Schnitzer's creativity in the same way that a brisk country walk may help a clergyman formulate a difficult sermon; the harder O'Shea worked the freer the inspiration flowed so that often a poem would come to him unbidden, ready to be jotted down. And Schnitzer worked like a coolie: even on the odd occasion when one of the two bricklayers he served, Bob Hawkins or Bert Wilson, told him to slow down because he was bringing them bricks and mortar faster than they could use them he would busy himself at some other task which he was not expected to do at all, stacking the planks and scaffolding tubes which others had left strewn about, or collecting brickbats and other rubble into a neat pile. It was as though he could not stand still for an instant so much did he enjoy his work and it was this bubbling enthusiasm that brought him up against the union site steward, a Corkman by the name of Pacelli Ignatius O'Mahoney.

O'Mahoney was a joiner by trade but his true vocation was for political life, the glamour of which appealed to him much more than the mundane business of first and second fixing; in later years he was to become editor of the ABU monthly journal, *Trowel & Templet,* and to stand unsuccessfully as a WUP (Workers United Party) candidate for Parliament. Pacelli Ignatius O'Mahoney had transferred his youthful devotion to the Catholic faith to the no less yielding tenets of Marxism and his role as a trade unionist, it must be feared, was nothing more than his own miniscule contribution to the world revolution. He had been observing Schnitzer's zeal for work with disfavour for some time and decided to have a word with him.

"A word in your ear, Brother," Pacelli said to Schnitzer one day as the poet slid down the ladder with his empty hod, eager to fill it up with bricks again. Schnitzer could not imagine what business the site steward could have with him for he paid his union dues without a murmur every Friday even though he had no particular wish to belong to a union at all. Up to now O'Shea had never belonged to any such organisation. It would have been inconceivable when he worked on the land at home in Glenbeg and the very notion of it would have aroused the Mule Kennedy to apoplectic fury.

"You seem to like your work," Pacelli remarked with distaste and innocently O'Shea agreed that he liked it very much indeed.

"I see," the site steward said grimly, his low opinion of Schnitzer plummetting lower still. Pacelli Ignatius had made himself known to Schnitzer the very first day that the poet began working for Consolidated Construction, asking if he intended to join the union. There was no closed-shop in operation, Pacelli explained with regret, but it was advisable to join just the same for strength lay only in unity. And Schnitzer, quite possibly misunderstanding the nature of the organisation he was being invited to join, agreed readily.

"Oh to be sure," he said, "aren't we all Irish?"

This was an unfortunate remark in the circumstances and in all fairness to O'Shea he was merely parrotting an expression he had picked up in the cable-gang; the poet himself never really subscribed to such clannish sentiments. O'Mahoney did not know this, of course, and he wrongly ascribed to Schnitzer a narrowness of outlook he never possessed.

"Nationality has nothing to do with it, Brother," he told the poet severely. "The Brotherhood of the Workers transcends all national divisions. May I ask where you worked up to now, Brother?"

Obligingly Schnitzer told the union steward that he had worked first for a farmer in the townland of Dromawn Aneerin and after that as a navvy in the Mule Kennedy's gang. That employment had been terminated for reasons which need not concern them, Schnitzer added, and Pacelli smiled bleakly.

"On the lump with the lumpen-proletariat," he jibed, but the quip was lost on Schnitzer, unschooled as he was in Marxist terminology. Pacelli then went on to give Schnitzer a little lecture on the benefits of union membership, on the obligation of workers to stand shoulder to shoulder in the class struggle and to develop the strategies which in time would enable them to control the means of production. It was a speech that was full of strange words that the poet would later repeat to himself, savouring their power and freshness, and of even stranger concepts, concepts that seemed to turn the world as Schnitzer knew it upside down. Nevertheless he forked out the enrolment fee required of him and, fearful that one of the high-ups would see him wasting time in conversation on his very first day, he made to resume working again. But O'Mahoney was not finished with him yet; Schnitzer must come to him if he had any little problems, should he be short in his wages or anything like that, or have any grievance, however small.

"And," said Pacelli, "if we don't get immediate satisfaction I'll call the men out and we'll close the job down like *that!*"

To emphasize the suddeness of the proposed stoppage Pacelli

54

Ignatius brought the palms of his hands together in a resounding smack, but the notion of such drastic action horrified the poet who would not wish to discommode the other men just because he himself had a grievance.

"Aw no, you sir.* I couldn't have that at all," Schnitzer said, aghast; and then for the second time in the course of that brief interview he gave voice to a sentiment not calculated to endear him to any trade-unionist.

"Don't grumble and stay: grumble and go!" Schnitzer said, repeating a favourite maxim of the Mule Kennedy whenever any member of his gang expressed dissatisfaction with the working conditions.

Appalled at this further example of reactionary thinking, Pacelli O'Mahoney shook his head sadly. "Well, Brother," he said to Schnitzer, "the fact that *you're* so deliriously happy in your work doesn't entitle you to ruin things for everyone else!"

Schnitzer did not know what the site steward was talking about and he said so; and, with a sigh, Pacelli began to explain. There was no justification at all, he told Schnitzer, for doing more work than you were paid to do: it merely hastened the completion of the job, swelled the bosses' profits, and made things bad for other men who might not be similarly inclined. The employer did not pay any more than he had to, so why should the worker do more than he need?

This line of reasoning had not been presented to Schnitzer before and he did not care for it at all. It seemed to him to be a negative attitude, inhibiting and ungenerous; cruel even, like hobbling a mettlesome cart-horse that was eager for work. Schnitzer was not the kind of man to begrudge his benefactor; he was being handsomely rewarded for his efforts, he believed, and if Consolidated Construction's profits increased in consequence of his labour that was no concern of his, in fact it was something to be proud of. Schnitzer attempted to convey his admittedly vague ideas on the relationship between labour and capital to Pacelli Ignatius who listened to him with growing distaste and finally told him that he was a political illiterate and a potential threat to the solidarity of the union

*A rather quaint form of address peculiar to Kilkenny and Waterford. Contrary to what might be imagined there are no overtones of servility in the expression; the English equivalent would be the egalitarian "mate".

and the class he belonged to.

"I'll be keeping a close watch on you, Brother," he warned the poet.

THE TENOR of Schnitzer O'Shea's life continued very evenly in Northmanton now and month followed month in blessed contentment. Schnitzer had the satisfaction of a job that he loved, he was earning more money than he could easily spend and the dozen or so picture houses in the town offered more films every week than he could possibly go to. He still sometimes wrote Anastasia Purcell's initials on scraps of paper – even tracing them on the quivering surface of the fresh mortar now and then – but he accepted now that she must remain "far, remote, like an evening star" and absence, contrary to the popular saying, does not always make the heart grow fonder. In short the poet's love for Big Ned's daughter dwindled to a faint glow that would never be quite extinguished but would not, on the other hand, cause him much more than an occasional pang. He did not, however, seek to put any other woman in her place but settled for the breathless contemplation of the beauties he saw on the screen, substituting art for life, as it were, and according each of the glamorous stars he admired a place of her own in the scale of his affections. Not to put too fine a point on it Schnitzer contented himself with the imaginary and if sometimes during the dead of night he called out the name of Rita Hayworth or Jane Russell or of any other such heavenly body there was no one to hear him but Ginger McGinn who slept through it all, snoring like a grampus.

Schnitzer got on better with Mother Perkins than any of the rest of her lodgers, most of whom only stayed on because, for all her barracking and unladylike language when she came home from the pub, she was more lenient in the matter of arrears than any other landlady in the area who took in working men. Schnitzer, of course, was always prompt with his payment of the digs' money and considerate in letting Mother Perkins know if he would have to work overtime and thus be late for his evening meal; it was a thoughtfulness she appreciated however much she might grumble at the time. Schnitzer, she often declared, was a cut above those other

56

bogmen who seemed to imagine that she had been put on this earth to slave her guts out for them.

It was only at work that there was any slight shadow on the poet's contentment and that only because of Pacelli O'Mahony's hostile interest in him. At first Pacelli was content to keep a watchful eye on O'Shea but when he found out that the young hod carrier was a poet, too, his interest took on a new dimension. Schnitzer, of course, would not willingly have let it be known that he wrote poetry for he rightly guessed that it was an activity that would serve only to alienate him from the other labourers on the site and especially from those who resented him because of his devotion to work. It was quite by chance that O'Mahoney discovered about Schnitzer's poetry and it was a discovery which the poet himself had cause to regret. Pacelli came on Schnitzer unexpectedly during the lunch break one day when the poet was seated on a pile of bricks writing something on a torn strip of cement bag, and with that suspiciousness of nature that characterised him he immediately concluded that Schnitzer was reckoning up his wages, that there had been a mistake made in the office if not an attempt to defraud O'Shea outright.

"Are you short in your pay, Brother?" he enquired hopefully, his nose quivering like that of a beagle when it scents the hare. It was an embarrassing moment for Schnitzer and he confessed, rather sheepishly, that in fact he was writing a bit of a poem.

"A poem, Brother!" said Pacelli, impressed. Pacelli was not without literary pretentions himself and he was already contributing articles of what he called a socio-political nature to *Trowel & Templet*, the organ of the ABU which he would later come to edit. Intrigued, he asked to read the composition and Schnitzer reluctantly handed over the strip of cement sack. The site steward read silently for a moment, his face registering flat disapproval, and in a voice that mocked the simple honesty of the lines he read aloud:

Mix the mortar, stack the bricks and fill the yawning hod
Feed the rumbling mixer till it spills
Climb the swaying ladder with your back straight as a rod
Serve the busy masons with a will!
Render thanks that's truly due, health's a priceless gift
There's no joy to equal work well done
Sing of strength and happiness as the dripping hod you lift

Turn your face with rapture to the sun!

"It's crap, Brother," Pacelli Ignatius said bluntly, "sheer unadulterated crap!" This was a judgement which Schnitzer would have been only too happy to let pass for he had never been disposed to discuss, much less defend, his own work; but the union steward had no intention of letting him off that easily. He was determined to make the poet see the erroneous nature of his thinking, the prostitution, as he saw it, of a talent however small. The verse was entirely devoid of any political or social consciousness, of any awareness at all that its author was a poor, exploited gobdaw* knocking his guts out for a pittance and enriching by the sweat that he shed the greedy crew that employed him. Could he not see that Consolidated Construction was growing fat like some obscene spider on the fruits of his toil? Could he not see that this drivel was exactly the kind of thing that the bosses approved of? It should be titled "The Song of the Happy Slave" O'Mahoney told Schnitzer in disgust and the only place it would be suitable for publication was in the firm's quarterly rag, Con-Con News.

Schnitzer retrieved with dignity the scrap of paper that Pacelli had contemptuously thrown on the ground and he would have returned to his hod carrying there and then but that the union man detained him.

"Look, Brother," Pacelli said with the martyred air of a sorely-tried mentor making one more effort to educate an arrant dunce, "do you not believe that you should put your poetical talent, such as it is, at the disposal of your class? Do you not think that your poems should reflect the realities of the class war, that they should be about injustice and exploitation, about the rotteness of the capitalist system?"

These were questions which Schnitzer could not even begin to answer for they were based on premises that he had not even begun to consider: namely, that the interests of employer and employee were diametrically opposed, and that the former was irrevocably committed to the oppression of the latter. So Schnitzer remained silent, and misreading his silence Pacelli renewed the attack. Schnitzer was a political innocent, he said (a slight amelioration of his earlier jibe!) but there was no

*Dublinese for a clown or clodhopper. It was in that city that O'Mahoney first came under the influence of Marxism.

reason at all why he must remain so, there were books aplenty which he would be only too glad to recommend, books that would enlighten Schnitzer to the true nature of society, the inherent conflict between capital and labour, books like *Marx for Beginners* and the *Workingman's Guide to Socialism*. These would do to cut his teeth on, so to speak, before he graduated to *How They Suck Us Dry* (a WUP publication) and the really gripping stuff like *Das Kapital* and *Lenin and The Fourth International*; it should be only a matter of time before Schnitzer's poetry began to reflect a true working-class consciousness, a proper understanding of the iniquities of the system, and a determination to smash it forever. There should be no further drooling about the joys of a job well done (a bourgeois concept, Pacelli explained) because the function of working-class poetry was to be a great cry of anger, a thunderous roar before which the bosses would quail in terror. The choice was his, Pacelli told him sternly: he could take his place in the honoured ranks of working-class writers like Robert Owen or Robert Tressell or the Donegalman Patrick McGill who himself had been a navvy: or he could remain a wretched little establishment hack, a lackey and a sell-out, a woolly-brained buffoon like Awley Mac Donnell* endlessly churning out piffle. The choice was his, Pacelli repeated, and walked off leaving the bemused O'Shea to contemplate these alternatives before loading up his hod again.

From then on the poet took good care not to be discovered communing with the Muse and whenever Pacelli O'Mahoney asked him how the poetry was coming along he pretended that inspiration had deserted him completely and that he couldn't write another line to save his life. Pacelli Ignatius was not so easily deceived, however, and his opinion of Schnitzer remained chronically low; it would have been lower still, indeed, if he had witnessed an event and conversation which took place some time later when O'Shea transgressed, albeit unwittingly, against one of the most hallowed of union agreements. It was a rainy day, too wet for outdoor work, and in

---

Compulsive jotter and diarist, author of Navvy's Notebook, Leaves from a Labourer's Diary, With Pick and Pen *and a ludicrous one-act play called* Navvies. *Though both natives of Kilkenny it was in Northmanton that they met for the first time as will be seen presently.*

accordance with the procedure laid down in the Working Rules Agreement (WRA) the men had "cabined-up" and were sitting in the site canteen playing cards and talking while the rain drummed softly on the tarred roof or wriggled down the window-panes like a plague of transparent worms. According to the WRA, which the ABU had wrung from the Building Employer's Federation (BEF), the men were permitted to sit around until two in the afternoon and if the weather showed no signs of improving then they were, not only free to go home, but paid "wet-time" into the bargain. It seemed an incredibly generous concession to Schnitzer, used as he was to conditions in the Mule Kennedy's gang where you either worked in the pouring rain or sat idle with consequent loss of earnings. But unlike the other men who could allay the boredom of being "cabined-up" with a game of brag or twenty fives, or a discussion on football, Schnitzer found this inactivity barely tolerable and so sometime towards mid-morning he slipped out of the canteen unnoticed and went round to the back of a tower-block where he began clearing up the materials that had been left carelessly about. Happy to have something to occupy him and untroubled by the falling rain he stacked scaffold planks neatly together, gathered swivel-clips and put-locks into tidy heaps and then he began digging a channel through the heavy mud so as to draw the surface water away to the adjacent drains. Wielding his shovel with consummate ease and uttering the odd shibboleth like "proletariat" or "dialectic" which he had picked up from the site steward he was happily unaware of the passing of time until he looked up to find the site manager regarding him with quiet approval.

Mr Mitchell had never spoken to Schnitzer before and of course Schnitzer had not spoken to him; a man of imposing appearance with his black-rimmed glasses, greying hair and expensive suit, Mr Mitchell spent most of his time in his office, but on rainy days, for reasons best known to himself, he liked to don safety helmet and wellingtons and to tramp all over the site, getting thoroughly wet while the workers stayed warm and dry in the canteen. Like Schnitzer, Mr Mitchell considered the wet-time arrangement a very philanthropic measure indeed and now he was agreeably surprised to find that at least one member of his workforce was not entirely unappreciative of his firm's benevolence. And in acknowledgement of this he greeted the poet with something akin to warmth.

"Doing a bit are we?" he asked Schnitzer; and Schnitzer, unsure whether Mr Mitchell approved or not, explained that he had become bored sitting in the canteen and that he would just as soon be tipping about at something. The site manager nodded understandingly; yes, yes, to be sure, he mused, adding that it was a pity that more men did not share this commendable attitude. The Irish, Mr Mitchell admitted, were pretty decent workmen by and large but there were signs that they were becoming infected with the prevailing selfishness, seeking unmerited increases and not putting their hearts into their work any more. In his youth, Mr Mitchell told Schnitzer in a burst of chumminess, working men put their heart into their work much more than they did today. It wasn't so much a case of "How much can I get?" in those days but rather of "How much can I do?" Job-satisfaction, Mr Mitchell said, was every bit as important as pay and he recalled how once as a boy down in his native Cambridgeshire he had seen a gang of Irish seasonal labourers – strapping chaps, they were – harvesting beet by the light of the moon! Now there was an inspiring sight, Mr Mitchell enthused, those fine Irish boys out there pulling sugar-beet by the light of the autumn moon while the locals were relaxing by their firesides or drinking ale in the pub! What a splendid example to the work-shy people of today! But then, the site manager sadly reflected before marching off through the mud again, you wouldn't even get an Irishman to do that now.

It was fortunate indeed for Schnitzer that Pacelli O'Mahoney was not privvy to this little scene for there is no doubt at all that he would have "blacked" the poet and brought the job to a halt to secure his dismissal. As it was O'Mahoney never forgave the poet for what he saw as his failure to identify with his class and employ his literary talent to further its interests. Commenting on this in his *Poet in Hobnails* Vidor T. Whitmere tells us that:

O'Shea's total lack of class consciousness was anathema to O'Mahoney with his hidebound ideologue's outlook; and when he failed to recruit the poet to his dehumanised socialistic creed the Corkman's chagrin knew no bounds. We know with what unflagging zeal the erstwhile joiner

61

pursued O'Shea in later years, castigating him at every opportunity in the intemperate language of the left. Rarely has any major poet of our time been subjected to so sustained a tirade of abuse.

Poor Schnitzer! Content with his lot in life, rejoicing in his strength of limb, and feeling (dare one say it?) a not unnatural sense of gratitude toward his employers: why *should* he have to trumpet a cause which he simply did not believe in? The poet did not feel used or exploited in any way nor did he see why he should become a mouthpiece for others. It was enough, surely, that in his first published collection of verse he celebrated the joys and sorrows of his young life and that later, in growing wisdom, he pondered the mysteries of human existence. Would he have served humanity better if he had done Pacelli O'Mahoney's bidding, read books like *Lenin and The Fourth International*, attended innumerable meetings in draughty halls and marched in every public demonstration of disaffection: if he had, in short, imposed on himself the blinkered vision of Comrade O'Mahoney who saw nothing in life but an endless vista of meetings, resolutions, strategies and agitations?

SCHNITZER ESTABLISHED himself so well with Consolidated Construction that he might well have had a job for life there but for an event which was to have the most far-reaching consequences for him, one of those malign twists of fate that offer no redress and which yet, in a strange way, may benefit others. It was two years since Schnitzer had begun work for Consolidated and he was employed on a different site now, on the erection of another tower block nearer the centre of town. It was on a Friday afternoon, almost quitting time, when the tragic event occurred. Bob Hawkins and Bert Wilson were pointing up the joints of the last two courses and down below Schnitzer was busily engaged in his end-of-day ritual, swilling out the mixer drum, cleaning the spotboards, dumping the excess mortar and tidying up a few scattered bricks. He had planned to visit the Picturedrome that night to see *Bloodlust of the Vampire*, treating himself to his customary tub of ice cream or quarter of jelly babies, with a supper of fish and chips on the way home; the quiet but happy routine that seldom varied but which he would never resume again. For, that night, Schnitzer would undergo the most complex surgery, fighting for his life on the operating table of St Chad's Royal Infirmary. Within seconds of knocking-off time, having done all there was to do below, Schnitzer went aloft to the fifth floor where the two bricklayers were putting away their kit and where, as ill-luck would have it, Bob Hawkins asked him to get rid of a spotboard in which a nail had somehow become embedded to the detriment of his large trowel.

"There's a good chap, Pat. Get rid of that spot, will you, or I shan't have a bleedin' trowel left," Bob Hawkins said, and obliging as ever Schnitzer picked up the offending spotboard to dispose of it. The construction industry safety regulations as set out in the WRA (section 9, paragraphs 3 and 4) stipulate that all materials be sent below on the hoist but it was common practice to drop unwanted objects down the lift shaft and, lamentably, this was what Schnitzer did, shouting "Below!" as a warning to anyone who might be working underneath. It is not clear, and neither was it firmly established at the subsequent court hearing, exactly how the accident happened; whether the poet slipped on the concrete floor, whether he overbalanced, or what. Bob Hawkins, in his evidence, said that Schnitzer appeared not to relinquish hold of the spotboard at all after shouting "Below!" and that he still seemed to be clutching it as he plummetted down the shaft; more damaging yet, perhaps, Bert Wilson told the court that in the instant before his fall "old Pat" had cried out "Kingston Bagpuize!" clear as a bell. All that is known for certain is that, through whatever cause, the poet dropped like a sack through the lift shaft to land in a crumpled mass at the bottom; and that when he was carried, unconscious, to the ambulance a few minutes later his workmates believed he was dead.

Chapter Six.

SCHNITZER SPENT SEVERAL months on the broad of his back in St Chad's Royal Infirmary swathed like a mummy in bandages, his left leg and his right arm in traction and with a variety of medicines and opiates being administered to him orally and intravenously before he was well enough to face the world again, albeit shakily, on a pair of National Health crutches. The poet's head required almost one hundred stitches and he underwent innumerable x-rays before it was ascertained that no irreparable brain damage had been done; it was all of a fortnight before he regained consciousness and almost a month before he recovered the power of speech. Indeed, it was nothing short of a miracle that Schnitzer survived at all and in the opinion of the operating surgeon, Mr Ranji Singh, his injuries were such as might well have killed an elephant; a handsome, if perhaps unfortunately worded tribute to the Glenbeg man's fine constitution!

Once the danger of death had passed and the slow process of recovery had begun the poet's natural energy clamoured for an outlet and he began to compose verse incessantly now, writing solely in the ancient and mellifluous language of the Gael which his grandfather, old Turlough Grace, had so fortuitously bequeathed to him. For whatever reason, O'Shea never wrote another word in English and whenever anyone asked him why this was so he would simply look at them in that unfathomable way in which his mother, Honoria Brophy-Grace, had looked at her questioners when she brought him home to Muldowneyscourt as a gurgling babe. Schnitzer was not only writing prolifically now, he was filling page after page with all the frantic urgency of some Victorian penny-a-liner, his cheap Woolworth's biro literally skimming across the page as copy-book after copybook was filled and consigned to the bulging locker beside his bed. Mother Perkins, who visited him every other day (though she grumbled mightily over the inconvenience) was hard put to keep him supplied with writing material – the cheap biros becoming exhausted almost as soon as the exercise books – and she remonstrated with him endlessly on the size of his output.

"Can't say as I see the point in it, boy," she would complain, helping herself to a pinch of the mentholated snuff she was so fond of. "I mean, 'strewth boy, what's it all *for*?"

But attached and all as he had become to his landlady Schnitzer did not feel impelled to discuss the force of his creative urge with her, and so the supply of paper and biros continued and the cleaning women complained more and more about the accumulation of copybooks in the locker. And O'Shea was reading voraciously too, mainly a thick volume of *Chambers Dictionary* which Lavinia Perkins had found one day while attempting to clear out the attic with a view to accommodating more lodgers. Not only did Schnitzer devour the etymological riches of its crammed pages but he transcribed many thousands of words thus making even greater demands on his harassed landlady who was hard put to keep him supplied with paper now. And Ginger McGinn, who visited Schnitzer on one occasion, bringing him along a fat bundle of old newspapers, was later astonished to find that his bedmate remembered almost every line and paragraph word-perfect. Apropos of this phenomenal improvement in the poet's powers of recall – and they had always been exceptionally good – the noted neuro-surgeon, Mr Barnstable-Walker, said that this branch of science was in its comparative infancy as yet and that there could be no cut-and-dried explanations for O'Shea's greatly enhanced memory. But there is no doubt at all that the poet's convalescence was accompanied by a terrific upsurge of mental activity and an overwhelming compulsion to create, a form of unconscious self-therapy in the opinion of Mr Barnstable-Walker, though it would seem equally reasonable, perhaps, to attribute it to his enforced idleness. Schnitzer O'Shea had never missed a day from work since he left school and never lain in bed later than seven o'clock in the morning so was it not a natural consequence of this that he could not now reconcile himself to doing nothing even in his weakened condition?

At all events he wrote and studied with a diligence that would put the most job-hungry student to shame, adding in a fever of acquisition to his storehouse of words and shaping poems with the speed of a potter moulding vessels on his wheel. And even at night, when the lights had been dimmed

66

and the ward had gone quiet, Schnitzer would lie awake reciting long litanies of the exciting new words he had garnered from the dictionary throughout the day. A night nurse came on him once, stringing words together in a rhythmic chant which she at first took to be some kind of prayer but which the poet told her was an "alphabetagam", a stimulating new verse form he had begun to experiment with. A little concerned, the night nurse recorded the incident in her report but it seems that nobody else thought it of any importance; later on, in circumstances which he could never have foreseen, the poet was to recite another "alphabetagam" to a television audience of millions.

And here one must consider an aspect of Schnitzer's character as a poet which has long intrigued, not to say baffled, his critics; his indifference to publication. Students of his work have argued over this and some critics have even gone so far as to say that his seeming indifference to seeing his poems in print was a sham, a coyness which had in it a strong element of rural cunning, the ploy of a countryman selling a cow at the fair and pretending not to care whether he got a buyer or not. And why, some asked with discernible envy, should O'Shea put himself out to have his work published when there were others only too eager to do it for him? There are, to be sure, writers galore who would not put pen to paper, however gifted they might feel themselves to be, without the inducement of having their work published but Schnitzer O'Shea wrote solely for the expression of his artistic urge and with no thought of anything more. "Full many a flower is born to blush unseen." Yes indeed, and it is a sobering thought that no line of O'Shea's poetry in Irish might ever have appeared in a book but for the agency of Cathal Ó Grianáin, an Ulsterman of whom it will be necessary to say something now.

Cathal Pádraig Ó Grianáin was one of the more controversial figures thrown up by the Irish language revival movement, a man of such unyielding conviction and unwavering purpose that he made enemies of those who would be his friends and gave ammunition to those who were his enemies. Cathal Ó Grianáin has been mocked and reviled by the rabidly anti-Irish Language Freedom Movement* as an intolerant crank, and insufferable busybody, and he has been dismissed by others as a harmless fanatic: but there is no denying that his life has been unselfishly devoted to the restoration of Irish, even to the extent of sacrificing a safe career in the civil service to that end. It was Ó Grianáin who first perceived the need of persuading the thousands of native Irish speakers who emigrated to Britain in the great post-war boom that they should not abandon their ancestral tongue, even when they had no prospect of returning to Ireland again. If the people of the Outer Hebrides and the Scottish Highlands could preserve their native language in the alien climate of Nova Scotia, and the Welsh exiles in far-off Patagonia likewise, could not the Irish in Kilburn or Moss Side retain their linguistic heritage too? So reasoned Ó Grianáin (a trifle optimistically, to be sure) and he forsook secure employment and an adequate pension in Dublin to follow the emigrants to Britain with that same kind of missionary zeal that makes some clergymen seek posting to the less salubrious corners of the earth. Cathal Ó Grianáin lived for varying periods in Manchester, Liverpool, Birmingham and Coventry before moving to London, Southampton and Luton in turn; and from Luton he went to Northmanton where he met with a singular lack of response among his compatriots, most of whom had apparently succumbed to that indifference to cultural affairs that characterized the people of the town. The Ulsterman became a familiar figure at Irish gatherings of every kind, in his thick Donegal tweeds and strong leather brogues, a gold *fáinne*** stuck in his lapel and his eyes gleaming enthusiastically behind his old-fashioned wire spectacles; he made it his business to get to know every Irish speaker wherever he happened to be and he strove valiantly to make them fulfil their sacred duty (as he saw it) of passing the Irish language on to their progeny, even to the extent of forming matrimonial alliances for that purpose. It was said of Cathal Ó Grianáin that he could, through some odd intuitive process, identify an Irish speaker even before that person opened his or her mouth,

* *Its membership was always miniscule but through skilful media manipulation and some well-publicized stunts it gained attention far beyond its relevance or importance. The LFM was supported mainly by ardent Anglophiles but as with the alleged funding of the* Irish Democrat *by the Kremlin there is no real evidence that it received any financial assistance from Westminster.*
** *A gold ring worn to denote fluency in Irish.*

and if this seems a little far-fetched it should be remembered that this was precisely how he made the acquaintance of Schnitzer, picking him out excitedly in the busy Northmanton market place one Saturday afternoon and button-holing him eagerly to confirm his hunch.

Schnitzer no more welcomed the attentions of the zealous Ulsterman than the many other men and women whom he pestered and he quickly became adept at keeping out of Ó Grianáin's way, resorting to all sorts of strategems to throw the latter off his trail. But, lying in a hospital ward, there was no chance of escape and before long the poet came to dread the visiting hours, eyeing the door of the ward with all the wariness of a cornered fox. For Ó Grianáin, with a totally mistaken sense of kindness, insisted on reading to Schnitzer the very kind of book which the poet would not have read himself. Gaelic literature has a strong leaning towards autobiography with a disproportionate number of books either written or dictated by non-literary people, small crofters, island fishermen or migrant labourers like Awley Mac Donnell, and this type of reading was not to Schnitzer's liking at all. Schnitzer's burgeoning intellect demanded something more substantial now than the homespun reflections of a gansey-clad islander or the mundane reminiscences of a Donegal tatie-picker, and the fact that Ó Grianáin's Ulster dialect was all but unintelligible to him made the ordeal of being read to less bearable still. (It also proved exceedingly annoying to Mother Perkins on the couple of occasions when her visits coincided with Ó Grianáin's – whom she immediately became convinced was a Jehovah's Witness intent on converting the poet!)

Of course it must be admitted that Ó Grianáin showed a certain lack of sensitivity by his insistence on reading to the poet but he meant well and when one considers that but for him no line of O'Shea's work might have come to light it seems churlish to complain. Cathal Ó Grianáin's primary concern was with the preservation of Irish and not with the thoughts and feelings which the poet expressed, and it is ironical that he who was responsible for bringing the poet's work to light should have been so unaware of its true value. Ó Grianáin, not to beat about the bush, would have sought to publish anything that Schnitzer might have written, irrespective of quality or content, just so long as it was in Irish.

And to admit this is not to diminish in the least the debt that Gaelic literature owes Cathal Ó Grianáin: if nothing else came of the Ulsterman's self-imposed exile but his discovery of Schnitzer O'Shea it would have been well worth while.

S CHNITZER'S LONG invalidity and the opportunity it offered him for thought and introspection wrought a great change in him; on his discharge from St Chad's Schnitzer had altered in a number of ways and not all, alas, for the better. Before his accident O'Shea had been reserved in company and slow to voice an opinion but now he was garrulous and assertive, much given to pontificating on a wide variety of topics and intruding quite often on the conversation of complete strangers to offer his opinion or correct them on some point. Allowances may be made for the impatience or irascibility that can manifest itself during convalescence when the patient's returning strength does not always match his will towards physical or mental activity, but this is more often a lapse from the normal state than a real aberration of character and it is to be feared that O'Shea's growing contrariness did not endear him to many.

One evening at Mother Perkin's dinner table a new lodger, a Cockney by the name of Alf Midgely, mistakenly stated that he had boarded the Princethorpe bus outside the Oxfam shop in Bradlaugh Street. The poet contradicted him flatly, asserting that the Princethorpe bus did not enter Bradlaugh Street at all and that to have boarded *any* bus outside the Oxfam shop would have been an illegal act since the designated stop was farther along, outside the Anglian Travel Agency, in fact! It was not a matter of any great importance and perhaps Alf Midgely might have let it pass, but Cockneys do not like being contradicted, especially by those whom they regard as country bumpkins, and he began rather unwisely to argue with O'Shea. *He* ought to know what bus he boarded and where, oughtn't he? A chap who had been a delivery-man in the Smoke wasn't likely to make a mistake about a thing like that, was he? Or to lose his bearings in a town that could be comfortably situated in the Borough of Southwark! And in any case, Alf Midgely concluded tartly, he didn't need a Paddy to put him right on things like bus stops!

This was an injudicious enough remark considering that the bulk of Mother Perkins lodgers were Irish and likely to resent the disparaging reference, but fortunately Schnitzer was more concerned with the falsity of the Cockney's claim and he went straight to the attack before any of his compatriots could take offence. A mite too cockily, perhaps, O'Shea asked the new lodger if he could name all the bus stops on the Town Centre to Princethorpe route and Alf Midgely replied that of course he couldn't and what earthly benefit would it be to him if he could?

"All knowledge is relevant, friend," Schnitzer replied, to the astonishment of the other lodgers who had never heard him speak like that before; and then, without a moment's hesitation, he proceeded to reel off not only all the stops along the route in question but the scheduled times of those stops as well!* Not content with that he gave a further display of virtuosity by enumerating the stops and stopping times along another half-a-dozen routes while his listeners stared at him in slack-jawed amazement. Thus did he effectively silence Alf Midgely who could only reply lamely that he hadn't got round to making a study of the timetables yet.

Schnitzer's easy disposal of his opponent raised him in the estimation of the other lodgers who up to now had tended hardly to notice him at all, but they soon wearied of his new aggressiveness, his readiness to quarrel over trivial matters and his assumption of near infallibility. His powers of recollection were truly remarkable now and modesty can be hard to practice when one is proved correct, again and again, in whatever point is being made. Some critics have made light of O'Shea's formidable memory, pointing to people like Leslie Welsh who was rarely ever stumped by a question relating to sport; but there is surely more to it, in the poet's case, than the ability to recall things with unerring ease for even in primitive societies men are trained to be the chroniclers of their tribal history, the repository of its lore. Would it be too fanciful to postulate that in cultivating so excellent a memory for arid and trivial knowledge O'Shea was seeking (vainly, perforce!) to encom-

---

* The source of this information was a tattered copy of the NTT (Northmanton Transport Timetable) which had lain for ages in the digs and which Schnitzer read over and over again.

71

pass that totality of knowledge, that chimera of omniscience, which had begun already to plague him? The notion merits more than outright rejection however unacceptable it may be in some quarters, but it was sad that this great upsurge of cerebral activity, this ceaseless questing for knowledge, should have been accompanied by the loss of the poet's earlier and more pleasing personality.

But genius is not always blessed with a smiling face and other equally regrettable changes had come over the poet; the sudden and inexplicable abandonment of the innocent pleasures of the cinema for the potentially ruinous ones of the public house. Schnitzer began to drink now, dropping into the Navvy's Rest (of all places) where he would sit for ages cogitating over his pint or attempting to get into conversation with his old workmates in the Mule Kennedy's gang who had been re-employed by that gentleman after he set himself up as a subcontractor, trading as Kwik-Dig Ltd. Schnitzer was less than successful in establishing chummy relations with the cable-men who were slow to forgive his former unsociability and in any case the topics of conversation which he sought to pursue did not interest them at all. One night, for instance, he put forward the intriguing speculation that it was futile to regret any course of action since action, once taken, could not be reversed. All acts were by their very nature irreversible, Schnitzer declared: once you had performed even so basic an act as blowing your nose you could not undo that act again. Or to bring the matter a little closer to home, since they were now all gathered here in the bar of the Navvy's Rest, it was inconceivable that they could be otherwise employed or situated: to remove even one of them from the scene as presently constituted would be akin to removing an integral piece of a jigsaw puzzle, the result would be incomplete. Whether the poet arrived at this proposition entirely on his own or whether he had already become familiar with the thinking of the Indian poet and mystic Rabindarath Tagore is perhaps neither here not there but it was greeted with truculent suspicion by the cable-men and one of them, Foot-iron Kelly, unmoved by the sight of the poet's aluminium crutches, asked what the hell he was bulling about? Schnitzer made a further effort to explain his line of thinking and added, with a sharpness that took the others aback for a moment, that surely

72

the subject was of greater interest than that which *they* had been discussing, the relative merits of steel-handled and wooden-handled shovels!

"Well just you buck your goat and we'll buck ours," the Mule Kennedy told Schnitzer coarsely and Schnitzer spunkily replied that whereas he himself could compare the durability of the respective types of shovel he feared that philosophical debate was a little beyond *them*. Things might well have turned ugly then had not the Guv'nor (whose facial muscles had long set in a horrid grimace from having to smile at the patrons he despised and detested) begged them not forget that an incapacitated man must be given some indulgence.

In fact the poet was making remarkable strides towards recovery now. If he could not yet go for those long walks which he took formerly he got about Northmanton surprisingly well on his crutches, from the pub to the public library and from there to the tree-lined park where he sometimes irritated and even alarmed senior citizens by asking them incomprehensible questions. Sometimes he would stand outside the Consolidated Construction site where he met his accident, wishing that he could reverse the irreversible and be back in there once more with his laden hod, fulfilling himself in honest toil. How deprived, how excluded the poet must have felt, as he watched the tower blocks nearing completion and hearkened longingly to the familiar sounds, the staccato bark of the jack-hammer, the whine of the power-saw, the boom of the compressor and the ring of steel on steel; how he must have cried out in silent anguish to be part of it all again, how he ached to sweat and strain and climb and carry once more, to feel that he had a role and function in life! Gazing disconsolately from without, Schnitzer would gladly have "turned back the heedles wheels of Time to happy days again" ("The Wheels of Time", *Milestones* pp 41 to 43) had that been at all possible.

Disabled, lonely and idle now, was it any wonder that O'Shea took to frequenting the Navvy's Rest and began to accompany Lavinia Perkins on her little forays to the Hope & Glory across the way? Those savings which had mounted so steadily while he was at work began more steadily to diminish now for Schnitzer's weekly sick-money barely paid for his lodgings, and so he went more and more to the post office to make withdrawals, but never deposits. On one regrettable occasion when he and Mother Perkins went along together to draw out some cash the counter clerk refused to pay him on the grounds that he was too intoxicated to know what he was doing and it is to be feared that the poet created a very unfavourable impression that day, striking the post office counter with one of his crutches and accusing the unfortunate clerk of unlawfully withholding the money.

But such unseemly behaviour was rare and it was not all booze and profligacy, not by a long shot. Schnitzer's interests were accumulating now with all the rapidity of bacilli multiplying under favourable conditions. Philosophy, literature, mysticism and even the minutiae of the most turgid official publications; to all these were now added a fascination with numbers that afforded him endless hours of comtemplation. The handicap of his meagre education in the Muldowneyscourt National School did not prevent O'Shea from appreciating the beauty which he perceived to lie in the certainty of mathematics, and the sense of wonder which he brought to the subject was more indicative of a lively intelligence than the mere ability to pass exams. To Schnitzer the infinite possibilities of mathematical reckoning resembled one of those clever cinematic devices whereby a rose endlessly opens out layer after layer of rich red petal yet never exposes the inmost core, or a doorway opens to reveal a doorway that similarly opens to reveal another doorway.

Such concepts excited Schnitzer immensely and one night as they sat in the public bar of the Hope & Glory he tried to impart to Mother Perkins some of this new-found perception of the simplicity and the complexity of numbers.

"Mother Perkins," Schnitzer asked, "have you ever thought about the immutability of numbers?"

"The what, Patrick?" his landlady enquired, the pinch of snuff she had been in the act of conveying to her nose suspended half-way for the moment.

"The *immutability* of numbers, Mother P."

This abbreviation of her surname Lavinia always found touching and she smiled with maternal fondness on the poet. "No, can't say I have, boy, can't say I have, come to think of it! The *what* of numbers, you say?"

"The immutability of numbers," Schnitzer repeated. "That which can not be altered or changed. Let me give you an

74

example."

"I wish you would, boy," Lavinia answered, with a returning hint of annoyance, "I wish you would for I'm blest if I know what you're getting at. Here, try a pinch of Daddy Rough!*"

"Right," said Schnitzer, eager for discussion. "Two and two make four: do they not?"

"Why yes of course, Patrick, what else could they make but four? Love a duck, boy, any kindergarten kid could tell you that, you don't need to be an Oxford graduate to know that, do you?"

"Agreed," Schnitzer answered equably, "so much for addition! But it's the same with multiplication and division and subtraction too, isn't it?"

"Why I'm sure it is, Pat, I'm sure it is!"

"Six times six makes thirty-six no matter how many times you work it out, and five from nine leaves four if you did it a million times over – no? And four into sixteen goes four times, right?"

"Well I ain't disputing that at all, boy, and I can't see why you're making such a thing of it, blest if I can," Mother Perkins replied querulously, but Schnitzer ploughed on regardless, asking if she did not recognize in the unshakable certainty of this a beauty entirely its own? If squares and rectangles and triangles and circles were said to possess the beauty of symmetry and form (as indeed they did) could not the *immutable* nature of numbers be said to constitute a beauty of its own too?

"You've lost me, Patrick," Lavinia snapped, quite irritated now. "I ain't with you at all, boy! Here, let me get a drink in."

But if Lavinia had hoped to divert Schnitzer's attention to other matters by the expedient of refilling their glasses she failed, because no sooner had she come back from the counter with the fresh drinks than he asked her if she had ever considered the finitude of numbers. (As a matter of mere interest the word that Schnitzer used was "finity" which, if philologically incorrect, conveyed pretty well what he had in mind, or would have done to someone more receptive than

* Cockney rhyming slang for snuff. Mother Perkins came from Camberwell Green originally and she like to retain those little characteristics of speech she had known from her childhood.

Mother Perkins.) Was there a finitude of numbers, did she think? And then, taking the speculation into the realms of philosophy, accepting that there had to be a finitude of numbers, be they stars in the sky or grains of sand on the sea-shore, would not such a finitude itself be too vast for computation even if it were theoretically possible?

The postulation was perfectly valid, if of no great immediacy, but here the poet had encroached on one of Lavinia's strongest prejudices: God's firmament should be left to him, she declared, and not be mucked about with by human beings however clever or educated they might believe themselves to be. The moon and the sun and all those millions of stars he was going on about, these were all the wonders of His creation, they were solely the concern of the Almighty and not to be meddled with as the bleeding Yanks and the Russians were doing now, putting dogs and things in space and talking about landing men on the moon.

"I shouldn't trouble myself too much about the stars if I was you, Patrick, you've got no call to worry about the stars. There's Someone up there has the stars in hand and He don't need no help from us mortals!"

But the pursuit of knowledge did not run contrary to God's wishes, Schnitzer objected, or why had He endowed us with the power of reason? And Lavinia, who could put a sharp edge on her tongue when she was rattled answered that she believed the Almighty had given us the power of reason to prevent us doing silly bleeding things like drinking Jeyes Fluid, for example, or walking under a bus. Or, should it come to that, falling down a blooming lift-shaft at work and ending up on crutches!

Schnitzer considered this dispassionately but before he could frame a suitable reply another regular in the Hope & Glory, a landlady by the name of Gladys Webb, intervened to say that her husband, Bert, believed the Yanks would put a man on the moon before very long. This observation was made in the mildest manner with no suggestion at all of argumentativeness, but the very notion outraged Mother Perkins and she rounded on Mrs Webb sharply.

"A man on the moon, Glad? A *man* on the *moon*? Don't you believe it, gal, not on your sweet life! God ain't mocked, Glad, and He ain't going to put up with that kind of nonsense, you mark my word. Not bloody likely, He ain't!" A trifle diffidently Gladys Webb remarked that she herself was not persuaded either way, she had only been repeating what Bert said; but the mere mention of Bert Webb infuriated Lavinia all the more and she poured further scorn on poor Gladys.

"Bert Webb?" Mother Perkins hooted in derision. "Bert Webb's as silly as backsides, always was and always will be! Your Bert ain't got the sense he was born with, Glad: that he ain't!" Understandably Mrs Webb did not take over-kindly to this and she replied with some dignity that her Bert might not be a genius but that he had been a good husband to her. Bert Webb had stuck by his missus, she affirmed proudly: not like some she could mention! This not entirely gratuitous reference was to Lavinia's spouse who had taken off for parts unknown many years before, being unable, it was said, to put up with the vagaries of her moods any longer. But the dig quite stumped Mother Perkins and it was a moment or two before she had rallied enough to take issue with Gladys again.

"T'ain't just because your Bert said it, Glad! I mean to say, gal, I wouldn't believe it was Tuesday if your Bert said so. That's how much gumption I think Bert Webb's got! But you see, Gladys, it just ain't so! Men on the moon, Glad? Cor blimey, gal, you don't think the good Lord is going to stand for that caper, do you? Never in a million years, Glad, you take it from me!"

"I don't know, I'm sure," the hapless Gladys murmured but Lavinia was subject to no such doubt.

"Well you take it from me, Gladys; God sees all, and he ain't going to allow a pack of silly bleedin' Yanks get ahead of him! Never!"

Gladys Webb contested the matter no further but the little difference of view had soured Mother Perkins and that night when she returned home she re-enacted her old theatrics, screaming up the stairs that she wanted everyone out at once, that she was putting the house up for sale and retiring to the Isle of Wight where there was an altogether nicer class of people. . .

✿✿✿ Chapter Seven. ✿✿✿

SCHNITZER'S RECOVERY PROCEEDED apace and before very long he had exchanged his metal crutches for a stout walking stick. To his many new preoccupations was now added another, equally compulsive one: he was frequently seized by an overwhelming longing to learn the identity of people whom he had known by sight at home in Ireland but whom he had never even spoken to in most cases. Long-forgotten faces from the past would suddenly loom before him, imploring identification; it might be the face of some man or woman he had seen among the crowd at a hurling match in Kilkenny of a Sunday afternoon, or of a farmer or cattle jobber on the Fair Green, or even that of some urchin selling newspapers on the street: but in every instance the face would haunt him for days while he yearned to know everything about its owner and was tormented by the realization that he probably never would.

Sometimes he would wake in the middle of the night while Ginger McGinn lay like a log beside him and wonder frantically about the identity of some person whom he remembered now with crystal clarity and whom he bitterly regretted not having got to know while he had had the chance. Who was the sad-faced man with the brown trilby and long black overcoat who always stood outside Pembroke's of High Street, or the horsey-looking old gent with the blotchy face and riding britches who never left the railings of the Ozanam House farther down? Or the old lady who cackled with such glee at the lubberly antics of the Three Stooges from the fourpenny seats in Tom's?* And (what was equally pertinent) why these sudden visitations, what caprice of the subconscious paraded these faces before him to the exclusion of others? Schnitzer pondered these mysteries and it was to Mother Perkins, as with so much else, that he turned in the hope of enlightenment.

* The Kilkenny Theatre, used also as a cinema in Schnitzer's time and called locally after the proprietor, Tom Stallard. An institution of considerable prestige, great actors like Garrick trod the boards there in their day.

"Mother P," Schnitzer asked one lunch-time in the bar of the Hope & Glory, "do you ever see faces?"

It wasn't one of Lavinia's better days for yet another of her boys had done a flit owing her a week's money; Lavinia Perkins, it must be said, lacked the necessary qualities for the successful pursuance of her profession and instead of insisting on prompt and regular payments from lodgers she frequently allowed them to get into debt; with the result that they often scarpered (as she phrased it) owing her money. Schnitzer's abstractions niggled Mother Perkins at the best of times but now, annoyed as she was at this latest example of perfidy, she felt little inclination to tolerate the poet's flights of fancy.

"Faces, Patrick? What *do* you mean, boy?"

"What I mean, Mother, is this: do you ever think of a particular face for no particular reason?"

"Cor, stone the crows, boy! Have you gone bonkers or something? What kind of a question is that to ask a body? Ain't I got enough on my plate with your sodding countrymen doing me down and not to have to try and answer daft questions like that?"

"Let me explain, Mother P," Schnitzer said patiently and, a little snappishly, Mother Perkins said she wished he would.

"Sometimes," said the poet, "I wake up in the middle of the night and there's a face before me, staring me in the eyes."

"Strewth!" Lavinia said in exasperation, taking a pinch of Daddy Rough but not offering any to Schnitzer.

"I don't mean physically, of course," the poet hastened to assure her, "It might even be the face of someone that's dead and buried for all I know – but there it is large as life before me, plaguing me."

"*Plaguing* you, Patrick?"

"Plaguing me because I can't put a name to it. I do be tantalized for days after, wishing I knew the name of the person's face, and not just the name but everything else about him. Can you understand that at all, Mother?"

"No, I bleedin' can't!" Lavinia retorted sharply. "Stuff and nonsense is what I call it, boy – you're reading too much, I always said you were, it ain't good for the mind, it ain't. You want to ask your doctor to give you summat to make you sleep, you ain't tired enough, that's what it is. The sooner you get back to work the better, boy!"

80

And there the matter rested for an hour or so, Lavinia flatly refusing to discuss it any further; but a little before closing time when the half dozen or so milk stouts had produced a mellowing in her attitude the poet brought it up again with rather more success.

"Mother P." he asked with engaging persistence, "do you never *ever* think of a face from long ago and wish that you knew whose face it was, and everything about the person?"

Thus pressed Mother Perkins admitted that come to think of it, yes, she sometimes, and for no reason at all she could think of, recalled an old seamstress she had known vaguely in her childhood, a little old Yiddisher gal who lived in Lambeth, it must be all of fifty years ago. But it was nothing special, like, nothing to get in a wax over, she wouldn't pretend for one moment that the old gal's face *plagued* her or anything like that. "Blimey, Patrick, I got too many *real* problems right now to worry my head over things like that, blest if I ain't."

Schnitzer was not so easily diverted from his own obsession, however, and he went on to tell her about the blotchy-faced old gent in the riding britches who mumbled to himself all day by the steps of Ozanam House, how he would dearly love to learn all about him before it was too late, if in fact it was not already too late.

"Well, if you're that keen to find out, boy," Mother Perkins said, regarding him through the spectacles that lay askew on her face, "why don't you pop over to the Emerald Isle and ask him yourself? Not as I believe he'd thank you for it!"

But this was hardly a feasible suggestion, the poet responded, he could scarcely make the journey to Ireland every time he was plagued by a face could he? And in the case of those deceased it would be a fruitless trip, anyway, barring he was to approach relatives who might conceivably resent his enquiries.

"Yes, I imagine they would," Lavinia said dryly. "Anyway, I can't see as it matters a great deal, I mean to say, the world's chock-a-block with folk we don't know, ain't it? Every time I come out of the house I see some face I don't know but I'm not going to get in a state about it, am I? Why, bless my soul, boy, if I was to get in a tizzy every time I remember a face I'd end up in the loony bin!"

But it was precisely the unattainability of the knowledge he so yearned for that tormented Schnitzer, the irrevocable nature of it. "It's the finality of the thing that bugs me, Mother. It seems terrible that a living person should be gone like a wisp of smoke or the steam from a kettle. Gone like they never existed!"

"So what would you have then, Patrick?" Lavinia asked, the sharpness returning to her voice again. "Do you want them to live forever? Blimey, boy, we'd be in a pretty pickle then, wouldn't we? The world wouldn't be big enough to hold us all, I'd have a queue as long as Watling Street outside my door a-beggin' for lodgings. I could charge what I liked, Patrick – and pick and choose, too!"

This rather unlikely prospect cheered Lavinia momentarily and the conversation then took a less vexatious trend; but Schnitzer's dementia persisted and would take an even more worrying form later on.

THERE MAY well have been some truth in Mother Perkins' remark that Schnitzer had too large a reserve of energy and that the sooner he got back to work the better, but it was certainly not from want of exercise for he walked miles every day now, twirling his walking stick jauntily as he strode along and uttering unfamiliar words aloud with an abandon he had never shown in public before. Even the walking stick he threw away before very long, though it stood him in good stead one night in the Navvy's Rest when one of the Kwik-Dig gang, an uncouth individual whom someone had nicknamed Popeye, sought to make fun of him by enquiring if he were in receipt of the old-age pension now that he had come to depend on a walking stick. O'Shea ignored the jibe with all the disdain of a Regency nobleman disregarding a whining beggar in Pall Mall and, piqued, the cable-navvy repeated the question, smirking at his own cleverness. By way of reply Schnitzer invited Popeye to consider the inalienable quality, the "isness", of things. Was it not a fact that nothing partook of the nature of a given object so much as that object itself? A milking stool was not a bicycle, nor a bicycle a beet-prong, and even if you dismembered these objects their very fragments retained the essence of the whole in a way that was quite remarkable. It need hardly be said that Popeye was not given to such metaphysical ponderings and by way of diverting attention from his

82

bewilderment he wondered aloud if deafness was not also the concommitant of old age (though not, to be sure, in so many words!) since O'Shea had not made any attempt to answer *his* question. The fellow was plainly bent on confrontation but the poet was prepared to suffer his rudeness a little longer. Perhaps, he suggested, the immutability of numbers had at some time commended itself to the other's imagination; that, or the concept of infinitude as applied to space and to matter. Was the human mind, he solicited, even equipped to grapple with the concept of infinity?

The only reply to all this from Popeye and the other members of the gang was a collective stare which conveyed apprehension and incomprehension in equal measure. The poet availed of their silence to try and explain infinity by quoting an example given by a Redemptorist preacher during a mission in Muldowneyscourt one year: that of a sparrow coming every thousand years to wipe its tiny beak on a towering granite mountain, and when the sparrow's beak had worn the huge mountain away eternity would not have even begun! Applying the same kind of gauge to spatial vastness Schnitzer begged them to consider the truly appalling notion of endless distance, of stars immeasurably remote from each other that were yet as close as two peas in a pod by comparison with other stars more infinitely remote still, if they would be so kind as to pardon the solecism!

"Shite," said Popeye coarsely. "You're talking a load of bull!"

At which the poet decided it was time to call a halt to the fellow's gallop and so, regarding him with distaste, he spoke the following little verse:

Hens squawk
dogs bark and
donkeys
bray.
Your harness needs
stitching,
my friend!

This last reference was to the torn pair of old corduroys worn by Popeye, and the spontaneous bark of laughter which it drew from the other Kwik-Dig employees must have hurt him deeply. At all events he made for Schnitzer, mouthing obscenities, and Schnitzer, with an agility barely credible in one just recovered from multiple injuries, stepped smartly to one side and brought his walking stick down with a resounding "thwack!" on the head of his assailant. Enraged, the bully wheeled round, fists flying, only to be side-stepped again by O'Shea who poked him contemptuously in the ribs with his stick before hitting him a stinging blow across the clavicle. The entire company was on its feet now, cheering and inciting, while even the Guv'nor who loathed all his customers equally was moved to concede that O'Shea displayed remarkable virtuosity in the use of the stick. Again and again Popeye charged at the poet and again and again the poet repulsed him with thrust and parry* until in the end, when it was clear that his attacker would not desist, Schnitzer yelled *Ipepecuanha!* and laid him out with a slashing blow.

But the poet was to lose a much more important battle, however: his action for compensation against Consolidated Construction. It was Pacelli Ignatius O'Mahoney who browbeat Schnitzer into taking the firm to court, of course, for left to himself the poet would not have done so. Schnitzer had the strength and resources of the ABU behind him, Pacelli argued, and it would be criminal to neglect this opportunity of making Consolidated Construction pay for his misfortune; the ABU would secure the services of a competent lawyer and O'Shea should have no trouble at all in relieving his erstwhile employer of a tidy sum. All the poet had to do was to make a decent impression, give the appearance of being a long way from recovery still and use a bit of common savvy when answering the firm's solicitor.

This, unfortunately, was exactly what the poet failed to do when he appeared in court, in fact his demeanour and looks suggested that he was in excellent fettle again as well as being irritatingly uncooperative. Mr William Ledgemore, for Consolidated Construction, argued very convincingly that O'Shea was the cause of his own mishap and not only that, but

* *Stick-fighting (with ashplant or blackthorn) was a common, if regrettable, feature of life in Glenbeg in the first half of the nineteenth century and a forebear of Schnitzer's, Cornelius Cuffe-Grace, was reputedly the most dexterous exponent of the art in the entire barony. Would it be too fanciful to suggest that the poet had inherited some of this ancient skill?*

in disposing of the unwanted spotboard (which was produced as an exhibit) by chucking it down the lift shaft, he had been in the most flagrant violation of the safety regulations; endangering not just his own life but that of his fellow workers also. Giving evidence on behalf of the prosecution, Pacelli O'Mahoney declared that nobody breached the safety regulations as laid out in the WRA more than the management itself, and that he had ascertained, within minutes of the accident, that there had been no handrail round the opening as per regulation but that one had been erected there almost before the unfortunate Brother O'Shea and been carted off to St Chad's! In fact, O'Mahoney asserted, if their employers had been intent on decimating the workforce they could hardly have skimped more on safety measures. It was nothing short of a miracle, Pacelli said, that there wasn't a major accident on the site every day.

Schnitzer, on the other hand, barely exerted himself at all on his own behalf, appearing to take only a minimal interest in the proceedings and thereby creating the very opposite of the good impression that O'Mahoney had urged. At one point he had to be asked, tartly, if he would kindly give the court his attention and, pressed for his account of how the accident befell him, he confessed with refreshing candour that he had been absorbed in his thoughts at the time and while he could remember very well what they had been about just then he could not say what it was that had caused him to fall. This was a very unhelpful admission, to be sure, and it is to be feared that Bert Wilson did not make matters much better when he declared that old Pat had cried out "Kingston Bagpuize!" in the instant before he disappeared down the shaft. The defence made a great deal of this statement and even more of the testimony of Mr Mitchell, the site manager, who told the court that he had always thought there was something odd about Schnitzer and that he had observed him on one occasion working out in the pouring rain while the rest of the men sat warm and dry inside.

Badgered and cross-questioned by the firm's lawyer as to the significance of the words "Kingston Bagpuize", the poet informed him that he didn't appear to be very well versed in the geography of his own country, that the place in question was a village in Berkshire and that he would have thought

85

a man who had been through university would have known that! The location of the village was irrelevant, the solicitor replied rather nastily; what he wanted to know was why Schnitzer uttered the words when he did. And in answer to this O'Shea remarked that the good people of Kingston Bagpuize might be entitled to some feelings of injured pride to be told that the location of their village was irrelevant; everything under the sun had some relevance to somebody, he suggested, and it was a form of intellectual arrogance to state otherwise. At this the defence lawyer shrugged his shoulders in a theatrical way and from that point on the poet declined to take any interest in the case which proceeded as though he were not present at all.

The outcome of it all was that Schnitzer was awarded a derisory compensation of fifty pounds and an incensed Pacelli O'Mahoney had to be restrained from physically attacking him outside on the courthouse steps because of his disastrous performance within. Was he some sort of collaborationist, deliberately scuttling his own case, the site steward demanded with perhaps understandable chagrin, or what did he hope to gain from such perfidy at all? If it was a job for life with Consolidated Construction he was after he would have got that anyway, irrespective of compensation, for it wasn't every day that the firm got hold of such a willing donkey as he, so what exactly was his angle in sabotaging the case? Anyone at all with an ounce of gumption would have taken Con-Con to the cleaners and here was he, thankful for a paltry fifty quid!

The poet bore all this with commendable dignity and, leaving Pacelli Ignatius fuming with rage, he went off in the company of Mother Perkins to cash his fifty-pound cheque and repair to the Hope & Glory where they remained until closing time.

B UT SCHNITZER was in for a more favourable turn of fortune now. The mound of poems which he had written at such hectic speed while recuperating in St Chad's had been despatched – at Cathal Ó Grianáin's insistence – to the Gaelic publishing firm of Banba Books in Dublin where the discerning poetry editor culled a selection of the best of them and sub-

mitted it to the *Oireachtas** Literary Competition. Assembled
under the collective title of *Milestones*, and with none of the
interesting dialectical variants altered or standardized,
Schnitzer's work easily took the first prize and Banba Books
very shrewdly brought out *Milestones* to coincide with the
Oireachtas itself thus creating a double event, the prize-giving
ceremony and the launching, from which the poet could
scarcely be absent. Review copies of *Milestones* went out in
advance and the impact it made on the majority of reviewers
was tremendous. "A fresh new voice in Gaelic poetry,"
enthused the *Irish Bookman* – adding, parenthetically, that the
adjectives were not always synonymous, – "Mr O'Shea is a
poet of great promise." "A clear and unjaundiced eye viewing
life with shrewd compassion and with none of the mawkishness
which is too often the sin of the writer in exile; Schnitzer
O'Shea has already secured for himself a respectable niche in
the ranks of modern Irish poets," wrote Farley McMahon in
The Sower, while in a long and rapturous review in *Aquarius*
Douglas Healey declared that Gaelic poetry had been given
back to the people by the young farm-labourer from Glenbeg.
"A primal voice untainted by modish influence ... O'Shea
will set trends, not follow them," Yolande Bevan predicted in
Distaff, and that most discerning of critics, Patrick Vandeleur,
writing in the *Crane Bag*, proclaimed an Irish Housman at
hand!

   Nor was interest in the poet confined to literary magazines
and the literary supplements of the national dailies: the down-
market *Sunday Pictorial* sent a reporter from its London office
to interview O'Shea and its next edition carried a picture of
him wandering round a ramshackle backstreet ripe for demolition, under a caption which ran, *Bard of the Backstreets*. "The
world of Gaelic poetry," the *Pictorial* told its semi-literate
readers, "did not die out with the Flight of the Earls. It lives in

---

* *An annual event comparable to the Welsh Eisteddfod or the Scottish Mod where
reputations are made and jealously guarded. There is a thriving oral and musical
side to it, too, and for a week each year the streets of the Capital resound to the
melodious Irish of Connemara, Donegal, Aran, Corkaguiney, Coolea,
Ballyvourney and Ring; not forgetting the new Gaeltacht of Co Meath where the
descendants of those banished by Cromwell now farm the rich lands their ancestors
were driven from so cruelly.*

the person of an unassuming Irish labourer in a decaying Victorian terrace deep in the heart of industrial Britain!" And in later years, Paddy Crookshank, the *Pictorial* reporter, claimed to have "discovered" O'Shea as though he himself were an intrepid explorer and the poet an uncharted geographical entity! If anyone discovered Schnitzer it was the Ulsterman Cathal Ó Grianáin, who considered the act as nothing less than his national duty.

Schnitzer's success called for celebration, Mother Perkins announced, and so on the evening of the day that a dozen complimentary copies of *Milestones* was delivered by a grumbling postman she and the poet paid a visit to the Hope & Glory where they began to drink beer and milk stout chased down by nips of brandy. It was at once a sad and a happy little outing for while Lavinia was tickled pink, as she put it, to have an author under her roof, it upset her that Schnitzer would be leaving shortly for Dublin to collect his *Oireachtas* prize and promote his book of poems with an appearance in the *Poets in Profile* television series. She would have been more upset still had she known how long it would be before she would meet "old Patrick", again. Nevertheless the celebration might have passed off happily enough but for the arrival, late in the evening, of the Ulsterman Cathal Ó Grianáin who had been hunting for the poet everywhere, eager to congratulate him on his success and to show him the fat roll of favourable reviews he had cut out from the various papers.

Ó Grianáin was a strict teetotaller although his work for the Irish language brought him into public houses often enough and now the suspicion with which Lavinia already regarded him was bolstered by his refusal to take anything stronger than a tomato juice. Nudging Schnitzer significantly she remarked in a loud aside that the good Lord himself hadn't been above drinking the odd glass of wine and wasn't it a knockout how some religious folk were so keen to take all the joy out of living? But most of all it was Ó Grianáin's refusal to speak English that really upset Mother Perkins.

"I say, mate, don't you know no English then?" Lavinia challenged the Ulsterman who with perhaps unnecessary hauteur corrected her little grammatical lapse and assured her that his knowledge of English was very thorough indeed.

"Well I should speak it then, chap! It ain't hardly the

height of etiquette to speak a foreign language when there's English people present, is it now?" Mother Perkins demanded huffily.

But here the poet intervened, chiding his landlady gently for calling Irish a foreign language, only to be rounded on by Cathal Ó Grianáin, aghast at O'Shea's lack of national consciousness.

"Och, certainly it's a foreign language as far as Mrs Perkins is concerned. Just as English is a foreign language to us."

And no less resolutely the poet objected: they could hardly call English a foreign language, even conceding that Mother Perkins was entitled to regard Irish as such. This touched a very raw nerve in Cathal Ó Grianáin who launched into an impassioned defence of that very foreignness to which the landlady had so correctly alluded; but, as so often happens with public-house discussions, this attempt to clarify matters only served to complicate them further, because Lavinia indignantly denied that she had ever *ever* suggested that the Irish were foreigners. Why, her own grandad, the dear Lord rest his soul, was Irish and if it came to that she considered herself Irish, too! It wasn't the Irish she objected to or she wouldn't have her house full of them, would she, but this sodding Irish language business!

"Say what you will, mate, but it ain't good manners to speak it in front of others," Lavinia concluded heatedly. "In fact it's downright bleedin' ignorant!"

Yes, countered Ó Grianáin quite sarcastically, that had always been the English attitude, it had characterized them wherever they went all over the globe: everybody must learn English to suit *them,* but would *they* condescend to learn anyone else's language? Oh, no!

"I shouldn't think so, neither!" Mother Perkins sniffed. "Let them buggers learn English, there's enough of them here!"

And the Welsh and the Scots and the Irish, they should all stick to English, too? the Ulsterman prompted with an irony that the landlady ignored.

"I should bloomin' hope so!" she snapped. "How else are they going to make themselves understood?" And anyway, she added, to Ó Grianáin's bewilderment, old Patrick had his own religious beliefs, being an RC, and he didn't need any of that old Jehovah's Witness lark!

His patience exhausted now, Ó Grianáin told Lavinia that Henry the Eighth would have been proud of her; a reference to the Tudor monarch's plans for the Anglicization of Ireland that was lost on Mother Perkins who, if she thought of King Hal at all, thought of him as a food-guzzling womanizer. The Ulsterman stood up to go, but as a parting shot he reminded Schnitzer that with their language so close to extinction the Irish could ill afford the kind of civility his landlady demanded. It was all right for the English, Ó Grianáin declared as he stalked off: *their* language was in no danger at all!

And then, with the irascibility of her nature, Mother Perkins turned on Schnitzer to vent her annoyance. "Just because some people write a book ain't no reason to get all high and mighty," she opined, helping herself liberally to snuff and rather pointedly excluding Schnitzer. "I mean to say, t'ain't even a *proper* language, is it Patrick? Not like English or French or German? More like ruddy Chinese, what I heard of it!"

Schnitzer, with a detachment that would have shocked Cathal Ó Grianáin, agreed that she was not altogether mistaken here, for Irish, in common with Welsh and other Celtic languages, did in fact originate in the East: or so his reading had informed him.

"It don't matter a button where it originated, I ain't going to learn it just to please old what's his name and that's for sure," Lavinia protested, close to tears now.

All in all it was not a very auspicious beginning to what was to prove one of the oddest phases of the poet's life; but being of a kindly disposition in spite of that assertiveness which had characterized him of late, he begged Lavinia not to distress herself and asked if she would not agree that every language seemed to have its roots in some other language: that just as English had derived from Latin and Saxon and French, every other language you could mention grew out of some earlier one?

"I've worked all my life," Lavinia complained, disregarding the origin of languages, "I've slaved and scrubbed and cooked: and what have I for it?" she asked Schnitzer.

"Work fills a vacuum in our lives," the poet replied philosophically. "Only in work do we find fulfilment." It was an

90

insensitive remark in the circumstances but the annoyance which Mother Perkins might have directed at Schnitzer found target in a less deserving quarter: Bert and Gladys Webb had just come in and Lavinia regarded them balefully before launching her attack.

"Patrick and I bin celebrating," she informed the Webbs with a sudden assumption of jollity. "Ain't we, old pal?" she urged Schnitzer, poking him with her elbow, and the poet agreed that they had.

"That's nice, I'm sure," Gladys Webb answered warily while Bert maintained his customary silence.

"Yes," Mother Perkins declared, "we've had a lovely evening! Old Pat's wrote a book of poetry, a proper book with shiny covers and all!"

"Oh," ventured Gladys hesitantly, unsure of what pitfalls lay ahead, "that's nice."

"Nice?" queried Lavinia sharply. "I should think it is! It ain't every day that someone writes a book."

"No, I suppose it ain't," Gladys Webb agreed uneasily.

"There's some as could never write a book, not in a million years! There's some," Lavinia persisted with a hard look at Bert, "who could hardly write out a bet, never mind a book!"

Bert Webb declined to respond to this reflection on the state of his literacy but Gladys was beginning to lose patience with Mother Perkins at last. "Why, I daresay there's people for everything, books or what have you. I daresay we could all write books if we'd got the time."

This opinion was greeted with a derisive little hoot by Lavinia and she leaned forward, her glasses dangerously aslant, like a hawk about to pounce on a sparrow. "Do you think so, Glad? Do you *really* think so, gal?"

"Well I dunno, I'm sure," Gladys faltered before the scorn of Lavinia's voice, "I expect we could."

"*Everybody*?" Lavinia probed with a supercilious little smirk.

"Most everybody," Gladys dug in, her resistance stiffening again.

Schnitzer intervened here to suggest that writing a book was no great attainment, that it ranked lower in the scale of achievement than any number of things he could reel off like a prayer. It was an honest opinion but Lavinia viewed it as little short of treachery. She threw the poet a pained look before

91

turning to Gladys again.

"So you think everyone could write a book then?"

"Just about," Gladys sniffed.

"My, my," Lavinia marvelled sarcastically, "there's a lot of clever folk about then!"

"Writing a book don't say you're clever," Gladys came back with spirit; and then, like a thorough ingrate, she glanced disdainfully at Schnitzer. "Blimey, Lavinia, you ain't going to tell me that old Patrick's clever? The Irish ain't noted for being clever, are they? Anything *but*, I should think!"

One can't assess how genuinely affronted Mother Perkins was, in a personal way, by this comment or how much of it was concern for Schnitzer; but she rounded on her opponent in fury. "Don't you dare call the Irish, Gladys Webb!" she barked. "The Irish are just as clever as everyone else, some of the cleverest people in the world are Irish!"

"Oh, I say, Lavinia!" Gladys Webb questioned amusedly. "I never heard that said before."

"Well p'raps you didn't Glad: I should think there's a lot of things *you* never heard of. You," she added in a barbed little afterthought, "and your precious Bert."

"You leave Bert out of it, Bert ain't said a word," Gladys retorted, looking reproachfully at Bert to emphasise the point. "Anyroad, Lavinia, I don't know what you're making such a fuss over, standing up for the Irish like that – you moan about them often enough!"

"Because I'm Irish too, that's why!" Lavinia told her and for the first time that evening Bert Webb joined in the conversation.

"I never knew you was Irish, Lavinia," he said in some surprise.

"And neither she ain't!" Gladys snapped in a tone that rebuked Bert's gullibility. "Just 'cause a body says something don't mean it's true. I could say I was French."

"I daresay you could, Glad, but you ain't," her husband replied with a hint of annoyance.

"No and neither is Lavinia Perkins Irish and I'm blest if I know why she says she is! You'd have thought there's enough *real* foreigners about these days without folk pretending to be things they ain't."

"Watch it, Gladys!" Mother Perkins warned sharply. "The

Irish ain't foreign, never were and never will be!" she declared. "My dear old grandad was Irish and nobody ever called *him* a foreigner!"

"P'raps not," Gladys conceded doubtfully; Bert Webb had retreated into his usual condition of apathy but now Schnitzer's interest was aroused.

"The concept of foreigness is a reciprocal one," he informed them. "In Gaelic the words 'foreigner' and 'English' are synonymous." And this observation, interesting as it may have been in itself, caught Mother Perkins offside, undermining her position even more than his previous remark; she had not been doing all that well against her adversary and she found it galling to have Schnitzer weigh in as he did.

"We ain't on about languages, Patrick," she reminded him sharply. "We're on about foreigners. Some folk," she said with a disparaging look at the Webbs, "don't know B from a bull's foot!"

"And some folk," Gladys Webb came back with equal asperity, "seem to know everything!"

It was more of a stalemate than a victory for either party but up to now Mrs Webb never had the courage to oppose Lavinia so firmly and Lavinia found the experience far from agreeable; the remainder of the evening passed in a kind of sullen truce but at closing time as they made their way home to Balaclava Terrace Mother Perkins' resentment boiled over like an untended saucepan.

"Fine friend *you* turned out to be, Patrick, siding with Gladys bleedin' Webb!"

"You misconstrue my remarks, Mother P," the poet replied with equanimity. "To agree with one is not necessarily to take sides. The most diverse and opposed factions may agree on a multitude of things."

But Mother Perkins was in no mood to accept the poet's equivocation (as she saw it) and she did not mince words. "Stuff and rubbish, Patrick – that's neither my arse nor my elbow! He that is not with me is against me saith the Lord, and you weren't with me when I was trying to put Gladys Webb in her bleedin' place."

"One would hope," Schnitzer retorted with perhaps unnecessary snootiness, "that a discussion could be carried on for its own sake and not as a vehicle for personal bias. Now if we may

93

re-examine the gravamen of your debate ... " But Mother Perkins was unprepared to do any such thing; she had the key in the lock of her front door already and in a moment she would begin yelling that she wanted everyone out ...

❧❧ Chapter Eight. ❧❧

SCHNITZER O'SHEA WAS quite unprepared for the acclaim and the welcome that awaited him on his return to Ireland. Four years earlier when he had sailed out from Dún Laoghaire on the creaking old *Princess Maude* he was just one of the many thousands who made up the sad exodus every year, a statistic in the records of an uncaring authority; now his seat had been booked for him on an Aer Lingus flight, his belongings were packed into a brand new suitcase and he had a telegram from the producer of *Poets in Profile* folded carefully in the breast pocket of his new suit. Then, no sooner had he passed through the customs and into the airport lounge than he was being paged on the intercom in tones of flattering urgency: "Would Mr Schnitzer O'Shea please go at once to the red telephone. The red telephone at once please, Mr O'Shea!"

Schnitzer, who had up to now never used a telephone of any sort whatever was confused, if not alarmed, but with some presence of mind he asked a passing air-hostess where he might find the instrument in question and the young lady, who wore a gold *fáinne* in the lapel of her smart green uniform, astounded him by whipping a copy of *Milestones* out of her shoulder-bag and beseeching him to autograph it for her. In something of a daze the poet obliged and the hostess bore him off proudly to the red telephone, chattering excitedly about his poetry and expressing the hope that they would meet sometime in Dublin. This was Schnitzer's first taste of that adulation which would be lavished on him in the coming weeks and when he picked up the red phone a soft female voice at the other end welcomed him to Ireland and enquired what sort of a trip he'd had; then, before he could even begin to describe the experience, the voice on the other end instructed him to proceed to the airport entrance where a taxi was waiting to take him to the television studios in Montrose. Still in a daze Schnitzer complied and the taxi whisked him away to Donnybrook and fame.

On the journey the taxi driver kept up a sustained monologue which Schnitzer largely ignored; it was, to be truthful, the poet's first real glimpse of his native capital for he had not seen much of it from the window of the train that had brought him to the mail boat four years ago and so while the taxi driver whined on and on about high unemployment and the rotten government the poet fed his eyes on the stately Georgian facades and the malodorous Liffey until they were in the suburbs again and nearing Montrose. Here Schnitzer tipped the driver handsomely and the young woman who had spoken to him on the phone greeted him with a smile and conducted him to the hospitality room where he was confronted with a greater variety of drinks than he had ever sampled before. The young woman anticipated the poet's wishes as his eyes roved speculatively over the assorted spirits and liqueurs, filling his empty glass each time with a generosity that verged on the reckless: thus it was that when Aengus Mac Proinsias arrived some time later he found the poet as responsive as if he had been marooned on a desert island and starved of the sound of a human voice. Beaming reassuringly and caressing his manicured hands, the presenter unleashed a torrent of Irish, a salutation couched in the kind of language calculated to put the Glenbeg man at ease.

"Arrah, Schnitzereen, you devil you, you oul son-of-a-gun! How in the world are you at all, at all, or how is the heathen Saxon treating you beyond in Cromwell's country? You're welcome, me oul son of Érin, a hundred thousand welcomes and the height of Knockmordawn* of congratulations to you. A major new poet!"

Even had the poet not been bursting to converse with someone all this would have had the desired effect for Mac Proinsias was wise in the ways of his profession; as it was Schnitzer proved a "natural" for the television camera, rising to the occasion with a panache that would have done credit to a seasoned performer. The rapport which Mac Proinsias established with his subject in those well-chosen few words flowered beautifully in the course of the programme as Schnitzer talked like one gifted with unparalleled fluency, never faltering or

*Cnoc Mordáin, *a forbidding mountain in Aengus's native Connemara. The felicity of his Gaelic greeting contrasts strongly with the more muted "Congrats!" of English idiom.*

hesitating for an instant as the words poured from his lips like water from a broken dam. Up to now few people had ever cared to listen to Schnitzer, far less pay him for the pleasure of hearing him talk, and so, eager as a beekeeper revealing the secrets of apiculture Schnitzer told Mac Proinsias of his early life in Glenbeg, of his fondness for the cinema and long bicycle rides after a hard day's work on the land; with flair and vivacity he spoke of his life in Northmanton, of Mother Perkins and the men she had lodging with her (though he omitted, with commendable discretion, to mention her little lapses from decorum) and, it must be said, he firmly but politely refused to indulge in such anti-English sentiments as Aengus sought to elicit in the course of the interview.

Under Mac Proinsias's judicious probing Schnitzer spoke of his grandfather, old Turlough Grace, and of Fintan Bolger who had so kindly provided him with food and shelter when he might otherwise have been packed off to an institution. He told graphically of his life in Britain, working first as a navvy in the Mule Kennedy's gang and later as a brickie's labourer for Consolidated Construction, and he told without a trace of self-pity of his accident and subsequent recovery. Had he been influenced by any particular poet? Aengus asked him, and with engaging candour O'Shea said that he couldn't have been exposed to any such influence since he had never read poetry; a reply that caught the interviewer unprepared for a brief moment as an errant squall might catch a slack-rigged sailing craft.

"No poetry at all?" Mac Phroinsias challenged with arched eyebrow, and Schnitzer confirmed this with an eager nod; poetry, as he knew it, was to be written, not read: he had never read a poem after he had written it much less would he read anyone else's poetry. In fact he believed there was more satisfaction to be gained from the contemplation of one quadratic equation than from the most elegant poem ever penned.

For one fleeting second the interviewer looked as though he wondered if the poet was having him on, but Schnitzer's sincerity was too patent to doubt and with the air of a driver avoiding a nasty jolt Aengus smiled and invited him to elaborate on the assertion. Nothing loth, the poet obliged.

"A mathematical proposition has the virtue of provability, it cannot be wrong and be right at the same time in a way that

97

a piece of poetry or a painting may be open to argument. Do you follow me?"

Gulping imperceptibly Mac Proinsias nodded and begged Schnitzer to proceed. "For example," O'Shea continued, in his element now, "arithmetical certainty has a beauty all of its own and nowhere else is the dictum 'Truth is beauty and beauty truth' more evident. The square root of nine is three, there's no disputing that, it's a fact and it's the truth. Truth and fact are not always the same in literature but there's no such uncertainty in arithmetic. You may argue about the merits of a poem but there's no denying that two and two make four or thirty-six plus thirty-six makes seventy-two. Or that seventy-two multiplied by seventy-two makes," – Schnitzer was obliged to pause for an instant and concentrate – "five thousand one hundred and eighty four! This is demonstrably so and therein lies the superiority of mathematics over poetry, however good!"

There may have been the merest suggestion of panic on Mac Proinsias's handsome countenance for the briefest of seconds but then, with an adroitness that was truly admirable, he diverted the conversation into more familiar channels and was rewarded later in the week by at least two very favourable reviews in the television commentary columns of the national dailies. "Aengus Mac Proinsias's stature as an interviewer was further enhanced by his latest appearance in the *Poets in Profile* series," said the *Irish Times*. "One watched, mesmerized, as with consummate skill he drew out the young labourer-poet O'Shea, encouraging him with a smile and a nod to ever greater revelation until in the end one felt that the poet had no choice but unburden himself in a flood of racy reminiscence. His little verbal vignettes, his unpatronizing view of his fellow-emigrants in Britain, not to mention his rather novel ideas on the superiority of mathematics to poetry: all this made rivetting television, an experience all too rare on the Box." The *Irish Press* spoke of Schnitzer's fetching innocence, what a welcome change it made from the phoney sophistication of so many of the other participants in the *Poets in Profile* series, while the *Irish Independent* paid tribute to the unassuming character of O'Shea. "The Glenbeg poet," said the *Independent*, "wisely eschewed the kind of literary ostentation, the vulgar show of erudition we have become so used to on programmes of this

98

type . . . there was no glib reference to Rabelais or Brecht, no smart quotations from Gide or Mallarmé. O'Shea was himself and that was enough."

At the *Oireachtas* prize-giving, where the poet went in the company of Aengus Mac Proinsias next day he came into contact with literary people for the first time in his life. Poets, novelists, dramatists, short-story writers and journalists of every kind milled about the imposing reception hall of the Mansion House, consuming great quantities of cold chicken-salad and even greater quantities of drink while chattering all the while with a volubility that rivalled Schnitzer's. Schnitzer O'Shea was a celebrity now, his hand wrung often and warmly, his work praised with equal warmth; and everybody seemed to attribute to him creative abilities he would never have claimed for himself.

"You must write a novel now," a young man with a sparse beard and glasses like the headlamps on a vintage Bentley told him. "The Irish emigrant working-class experience has never been fully articulated, not even by Patrick MacGill. You must be the voice of the voiceless now!"

"You must write a play for the Abbey," a silver-haired man wearing a speckled bow-tie and claret-coloured waistcoat insisted. "Your theme can be the angst of the Irish exile in Britain."

Another autobiography on the lines of Awley Mac Donnell's *Navvy's Notebook* would not come amiss, either, a small publisher told the poet. It had become fashionable to deride that genre but it sold well all the same. Somebody else advised him to keep a diary, observing that whereas only the very best of literature could hope to endure, a diary, as a social document, would be read by generations yet unborn.

At the prize-giving itself Schnitzer was accorded an exceptional measure of applause and the Master of Ceremonies, Dualtach Mac Giolla Phádraig, made a brief speech in which he said that while it was a tragedy that young men of such talent had to leave their homeland in search of a living there was the consolation of knowing that in Schnitzer O'Shea they had the best kind of ambassador, one who would bring nothing but credit to *Clanna Gael**. He was, moreover, living proof of

*Literally, "the Gaelic family", or clan.

the indestructibility, the tenacity, of our ancient culture, a link in a sterling chain.

It was a most memorable evening and if Schnitzer over-indulged in the refreshments so freely purveyed (as well as in an orgy of conversation) it would be an ungenerous soul that grudged him his hour of glory. There is no point in seeking to conceal it, for it is a matter of record now, that just before the conclusion of the festivities a little before midnight, and while a well-known television producer was urging him to appear on his show, the poet's legs suddenly buckled and he slumped, unconscious, to the floor.

SCHNITZER STAYED, courtesy of Radio Telefís Éireann, for two nights at the Montrose Hotel where he had not just a bed, but a room all to himself, amid such comfort and luxury as he had experienced only vicariously up to now on the cinema screen. He was to have returned to Northmanton after the launching of *Milestones* but Aengus Mac Proinsias it was who dissuaded him.

"Any able-bodied man at all can hump bricks or dig holes, Schnitzereen," Mac Proinsias suggested, "but few have the gift of poetry. You must stay here in Ireland and write!"

Schnitzer stayed but he did not write, and he found accommodation in 6 Harcourt Villas in one of the better inner suburbs. Schnitzer's new lodgings differed from his previous ones both in the character of the boarders and that of the proprietor, Mrs Concepta Fitzgerald. Mrs Fitzgerald catered for clerical workers of various grades, civil servants mainly, and unlike Mother Perkins she did not encourage familiarity nor extend them grace in the matter of payment. Less still did she tolerate any obvious signs of drunkeness: the guest (Concepta Fitzgerald considered the term "lodger" common) who wobbled even slightly as he approached her door was in for a severe reprimand and if he did not mend his ways would soon be asked to find other accommodation. Mrs Fitzgerald did not subscribe to the traditional Irishwoman's view that drink was the good man's failing but most of her guests had the civil servant's faculty of appearing sober even when well soused and so she did not make too great a fuss. Schnitzer managed not to run foul of her until one night he created a rumpus which will be dealt with in due course but she never warmed to him as Mother Perkins had done and since her outings were confined to evening devotions in the many churches of the city there was little likelihood of his getting to know her socially. Nor did the poet himself take very much to his fellow guests in Harcourt Villas. They were a dispirited lot, it seemed to Schnitzer, eating their meals in gloomy silence in the chilly dining-room under the glassy stare of a stuffed fox, conversing in monosyllables for the most part and then only to make unfavourable comment on the quality of the food. Schnitzer's attempts at conversation were not only unwelcome but were brusquely rebuffed; his status as a poet did not impress the civil servants and even had he been gifted with the charm and wit of Oscar Wilde he would have found them coldly unreceptive over their corn flakes and fried eggs.

But Schnitzer was absent for most other meals, living a life so full now that there seemed scarcely enough hours in the day. He was in frequent demand on radio and television and in rapid succession he appeared on a number of programmes as varied in tone and content as *Hot Seat, Talking Point, Relics, Perceptions, Whizz-Go* and *Focus* to name but a few. That O'Shea contributed little of value to any of these entertainments must be admitted for he seemed hypnotized by the sound of his own voice now and he prattled on relentlessly whether he had anything of consequence to say or not. Indeed O'Shea very often disregarded whatever question was being put to him, proffering his own reflections instead on such disparate matters as the concept of infinitude and the "isness" of objects! Yet strangely the invitations continued so that apart from the advances that Banba Books paid him on his collection of poems no week went by but some cheques arrived for him in the post. And when he wasn't being paid to talk on radio or television Schnitzer was talking with equal willingness in those public houses that were the haunts of the literati, Davy Byrnes, or McDaids, Mulligan's of Poolbeg Street or the Pearl Bar. For the poet was now enmeshed in what Hiram S. Walbark called "the Liffey syndrome": the endless round of pub conversations that are never planned or intended but grow naturally out of occasion and circumstance, waxing and waning throughout the day as the company swells and diminishes like a fire that dwindles until tended again. It was a mode

101

of life that O'Shea found immensely diverting and if he proved a more eager speaker than a listener he was no different from those others who spent their time in this way.

But of course it was all quite unproductive for O'Shea had not written so much as a line since coming to Dublin nor would he for the length of his stay there. Rónán Mac Rónáin, the poetry editor of Banba Books, was alert to this danger from the moment the poet set foot in Dublin and he lost no time in warning Schnitzer. He would never produce any work while he consorted with the pub talkers, Mac Rónáin told Schnitzer, and in time he would become chronically infected with their inertia.

"Go back to Britain," he advised Schnitzer one night in Madigan's of Moore Street. "You'll never write anything here."

But since the poet showed no signs of accepting this wise counsel Mac Rónáin later urged him to lock himself away in his room for several hours each day with pen and paper on the table before him. Why, asked Mac Rónáin, if he could compose poetry with the rasp of a concrete mixer in his ears could he not do so in the quiet of his bedroom? Or better still rent a small cottage in the country somewhere, in the seclusion of the Dublin mountains or in the isolation of a Leitrim bog; anything but to waste his time in incessant, sterile talking. This waste of literary ability was something which Rónán Mac Rónáin had long deplored and though he moderated his views in later years he was remembered for his not entirely serious advocacy of a form of detention for writers in Irish, a government-sponsored scheme that would produce a bumper crop of novels, short stories and plays. Writers, Mac Rónáin believed, had a tendency towards laziness, but whereas the major languages could tolerate this Irish needed some positive discrimination in its favour if it was to flourish at all. And, he maintained, just as in wartime when civil liberties may be curtailed or suspended for the common good, in a situation of such gravity as faced the Gaelic tongue it was morally permissible to do whatever might be necessary for its preservation. Thus an encampment of some sort – preferably in a remote area with few distractions – where a couple of hundred writers, major and minor alike, could be accommodated in reasonable comfort seemed to him a worthwhile idea. Surely with the discipline of a healthy and regular life (*mens sana in corpore sano!*) the creative genius would be stimulated to fruitful expression? And was not the comparative loss of freedom for a relatively brief spell a small sacrifice to make for so worthy a cause? Writers could regard it as a form of national service of the highest order.

It need scarcely be said that this excess of zeal on the part of Mac Rónáin was seized upon delightedly by the Language Freedom Movement (so-called) and its Anglophile supporters as further evidence of the fascism inherent in Irish nationalism, and terms of abuse like "elitism" and "herrenvolk" were tossed about with abandon; Rónán Mac Rónáin defended himself with vigour, pointing out that contrary to the innuendo put about by his detractors in the LFM he had never said a word about things like guard dogs or armed guards at all, nor searchlights or barbed wire either! However, nothing more was heard of Mac Rónáin's detention scheme which was just as well; one cannot imagine O'Shea benefitting from such coercion, whatever about taking a rented cottage.

Meanwhile, over in Britain, Pacelli Ignatius O'Mahoney was keeping a cold eye on Schnitzer's rise to fame. The union steward was especially scathing about what he saw as Schnitzer's eagerness to savour the fruits of success. "The Bard of the Backstreets," he sneered in a waspish contribution to *Trowel & Templet,* "could hardly wait to play the role assigned him by the bourgeois literati of Dublin to posture and babble on television, a token worker in a middle-class milieu. O'Shea, as the possessor of some small talent might have used his gifts (such as they are) in the service of his class, but he chose the fleshpots instead and he has paid the price. In the world of working-class writing O'Shea is an irrelevancy now."

The poet was anything but irrelevant in Dublin, however, for he was fast becoming something of a cult figure and already the influence of *Milestones* was reflected in some of the verses published in the monthly literary magazines, *Comhar* and *Feasta,* while eager young poets flocked to whatever watering-place it might be where Schnitzer was imbibing. Many of his most inconsequential remarks were seized upon avidly now and propagated tirelessly wherever writers and those who basked in the atmosphere of writing foregathered. O'Shea was an iconoclast, some claimed, while others saw him as a realist of unflinching integrity, one who looked on life with a terrifying clarity. Nor was it surprising that the poet was seen variously as a maverick, a nihilist and any other number of things that did not fit into those categories to which his public would consign him. A labouring man with no sense of working-class affinity, an Irish speaker who regarded his native language as being of neither greater nor lesser importance than English, a poet who believed poetry to be inferior to many other branches of mental endeavour and above all, perhaps, a man with an insatiable craving for knowledge of the most diverse and even useless nature. Was it any wonder that people should be at a loss when confronted with the embodiment of so many contradictions?

And of course the poet's multi-faceted personality together with his fearless exposition of so many unorthodox views gained him an entrée to circles where most of his fellow poets would neither have gone nor been welcome; O'Shea, after a day's drinking, ended up at many a gathering where the nature and quality of his poetry were the farthest things from the minds of the philistine social-climbers knocking back their pink gins and martinis. It was at one such affair that the contractor, Mr Patrick (Paddy) Mulligan of Mulligan Dwellings rather patronizingly told Schnitzer that he would give him a job carrying the hod on a Mulligan site if the old poetry racket ever gave out but, bejazez, he'd have to work hard there for there were no dossers employed by Mulligan Dwellings! The yelp of sychophantic laughter that greeted this little sally gave way to an embarrassed silence when Schnitzer thanked the building contractor and promised that if the bottom ever fell out of the jerry-building game and Mr Mulligan was feeling the pinch he might be able to get him a job in the Mule Kennedy's gang which, the poet added, ought to suit him as the Mule was a great believer in hard work, too!

And it was at another, though admittedly more cultured gathering – the launching of Donna Lacey's atrocious book on Ireland and the Irish, *They Never Say Begorrah!* – that Schnitzer became entangled in another fracas, this time with the author when he quite inadvertently spoke to her in Irish and she snapped furiously "Stop speaking that gibberish!" The soul of toleration, particularly in linguistic matters, O'Shea was careful not to address Ms Lacy in Irish again but the affront

104

lingered and in her next book, *The Mohair Mahoons*, (which purported to be a study of the Irish *nouveau riche*) she gave a rather different version of the encounter: "A rather gauche young man, O'Shea blushed to the roots of his spiky hair, kneading his stubby workman's fingers in an agony of embarrassment, when I chided him gently for speaking to me in Gaelic, a ludicrous language with which I had no intention of becoming acquainted."

But the poet was revelling in his new life now, it was still a tremendous novelty to find people only too willing to listen to him when at the dinner table in Mother Perkins' house he had so often been told to shut up; every day he awoke now was an adventure that stretched before him and beckoned seductively, a long stimulating day when the ideas that came to him as thick as snowflakes in a blizzard could be aired in the congenial atmosphere of the pub. "Guru" is perhaps an inapplicable word in this context for there was no trace of the messianic in the poet's discourse, but a man of less character might easily have been carried away by the deference shown to him by so many, particularly by the duffel-coated and scarved students of literature from Trinity College and UCD.

O'Shea, the farm-labourer from Dromawn Aneerin, had come a long way.

❧❧ *Chapter Nine.* ❧❧

THE LIFE THAT O'Shea was leading now, however satisfying it may have been, was not without its attendant dangers. It was an unhealthy life by comparison with that of the farm and the navvy gang and it need hardly be said that constant exposure to tobacco-filled air and lack of exercise – not to mention over-indulgence in alcohol – must take their toll of the strongest constitution. There was no cycling for Schnitzer now though he could well have got himself a bike, no muscle-toning labour nor long walks even, such as had helped him to recovery in Northmantton. Instead the poet spent most of his waking hours in the pub or in radio and television studios where the light of day never penetrated; not surprisingly he grew stout, if not obese, and his energy became almost wholly mental so that while he could debate or discourse until the cows came home with no sign of wearying, his bodily vigour seemed to have left him altogether.

But it is to be feared that the poet's deterioration was not of the body alone. He began to show signs of nerviness, growing daily more irritable and argumentative and developing certain little peculiarities of behaviour; a compulsion, for example, to collect every spent matchstick within reach and break it into tiny fragments. Later on, beermats and cigarette cartons became the object of his attention too, and these he would tear into minute shreds before assembling them in a pile on an ashtray and setting them alight. Such activity may have been no more than a symptom of stress, like a nervous tic, and equally unconscious, for often even in the middle of an animated discussion Schnitzer would disappear beneath the table to retrieve a matchstick without a pause in whatever he might be saying just then. But there were other portents, too. One night he sat with Rónán Mac Rónáin over a quiet drink in a pub they did not visit often, and while Mac Rónáin was urging him once more to rent a little cottage in the country, Schnitzer quite unexpectedly cried *Hackballscross!* in a loud voice. Mac Rónáin was taken aback, to say the least, but with that tact which is the mark of the true gentleman, he affected not to notice. But he became convinced that the poet himself and not just his art would benefit from a spell of quiet far away from the distractions of the capital.

Schnitzer, however, showed no sign at all of wanting to leave Dublin, not even to take the two and a half hour's bus-ride down to Glenbeg where he had become a source of great pride to everyone with the exception of Big Ned Purcell and one or two more of that ilk. Hiram S. Walbark in his *Schnitzer O'Shea, Man and Myth* makes much of Schnitzer's refusal to visit the scenes of his childhood (the television series *Féach* sought to bring him there to make a programme) and expounds the idea that the poet had written his native place out of his system in *Milestones*. There may be a grain of truth in that but surely Schnitzer himself gives the reason in that fine fragment "There's No Going Back" (*Milestones* p 83):

> There's no going
> back
> there never
> was
> wanting to go
> back
> is like wanting to
> be born
> again.

There was nothing for Schnitzer in Muldowneyscourt or in Dromawn Aneerin any more for Anastasia Purcell had married and he would hardly wish to go to work for Fintan Bolger as a farm labourer again. All he would find in Glenbeg, perhaps, was the revival of a painful memory and he was mature enough to let the past be gone.

But neither could the poet continue forever in the mode of life he had known since coming to Dublin and it was a chance encounter at a convention of Irish – that is Gaelic – writers in the Mansion House which really began the process of alienation that would cause Schnitzer to shun the company of literary men and eventually to return to Britain. The Gaelic literary scene, claustrophobically small by comparison with Irish writing in English, was nevertheless riven with jealousies and divisions, reputations being savaged with all the ferocity of the Crusades and guarded with equal zeal; writers who

108

should have been united in the interests of their chosen medium attacked one another with more relish than they attacked those who wrote in English. O'Shea was quite unaffected by all this (if he was more than passingly aware of it) but at the convention Aengus Mac Proinsias dragged him along to his education commenced in a quite startling manner.

The meeting was very well attended and varied in composition from old pipe-smoking stalwarts of the early days of the Language Revival to impatient young men hellbent on revolutionising Irish writing, and no sooner was the agenda gone through with the customary amount of wrangling and hairsplitting than a bitter argument broke out between two novelists as to what direction Gaelic writing should take. The antagonists were Iarmaid Ó Dúláin whose newly-published novel *Na Feidhleacháin** had created a sensation even greater than the publication of *Milestones,* and Caitríona** who had also just published another novel, his fifty-fifth; a very readable, if somewhat familiar, tale of life on the western seaboard, the struggle for existence among the rocks and moorland at home and the no less harsh living of the tunnel-men and tatiehokers who emigrated to Scotland. Ó Dúláin's novel dropped like a mighty boulder into a placid pool, sending out waves of response that varied from splenetic fury to joyous acclaim. Traditionalists screamed that the language had been prostituted for the sake of tawdry modernism and made to portray a way of life that was alien to those cherished ideals handed down from generations long dead, while the avant-garde declared that The Butterflies had dragged Gaelic fiction, screaming, into the latter half of the twentieth century where it surely belonged if it was to have any relevance to modern life. Was the language to be confined to the ghetto forever, restricted to the scattered inhabitants of bog and rocky coast? Must Irish never come to grips with the complexities of

*Literally "The Butterflies" but more aptly, in modern parlance, "The Beautiful People". This was the first work of fiction in Irish to deal with the lifestyle of the new entrepreneurial class in the Irish capital. Predictably it drew howls of anguish from the traditionalists who did not regard the subject a fit one for Gaelic literature.

**Many of the older generation of Gaelic writers had a fondness for pen-names that were either womens' first names ("Caitríona" was a man!) or were ornithic in origin, e.g. The Crested Grebe, of whom more shortly.

modern living; the hot-dog stand, the pool-room, the laundromat and the parking-meter? Should they turn their backs on the reality of present-day industrialised Ireland, the exciting new Ireland of the vast council-house estates and the exclusive millionaires' rows, for the stale and arid dream of the thatched cabin and the donkey-cart? Nobody had written in Irish about the smart set, the martini-drinkers and the wheeler-dealers until Ó Dúláin had done so; it was a most auspicious beginning indeed but it must be just a beginning and they must go on to explore every single facet of modern Irish life as fearlessly and as honestly as if they were writing in the language of the majority. To hell with the caubeen* and the three-legged pot: bring on the cocktail-shaker and the Pill! And the Lamborghini!

The opposition was even more voluble, if anything. *An Craoibhín Bláfar*** would turn in his grave if he could see what misuse was being made of the language he had given his life to preserving, the language that had reached full bloom long before the Saxon and Norman tongues begat the amalgam that we know as English today! Irish enshrined all that was best and noble in the life of the nation and why pervert its unrivalled imagery to portray all that was rotten and sordid in the modern world. The towns and cities had no monopoly on reality, the traditionalists bawled: the donkey-cart was no less real than your Italian sportscar and a *taoscán**** of poteen was better than all the martinis in Dublin; *and* our forefathers had managed alright without the curse-of-God Pill, thank you! Money and not idealism was what motivated the publishers of *Butterflies*, the supporters of Caitríona accused, and at this the publisher of *Butterflies* jeered derisively that if money was his object he'd be better employed digging ditches beyond in Britain which, he suggested quite bluntly, was where some of his detractors ought to be! This only infuriated the opposition all the more and there were cries of "*Bás roimh striapachas!*" (Death before prostitution!) and "Muck-merchants!"

*Cáibín, *an old hat, generally of soft material; like the three-legged pot it symbolizes an aspect of rural Ireland.*
**The Blossoming Branch, *nom-de-plume of one of the most devoted early revivalists. At the age of twenty-four he took a vow never to speak a word of English again and kept it until his demise as an advanced nonogenarian!*
*** A (*usually generous*) measure of drink.

countered by shrill yells of "Ostriches!" and "Antiquarians!" from the moderns.

It was at this stage in the proceedings that the chairman managed to enforce some order but before he could get the meeting under way again the author of *Butterflies* vaulted lightly onto the rostrum, grabbed the microphone from the chairman and announced that he had something to say. No writer should be called on to explain or defend his work, Ó Dúláin declared, and he certainly did not intend doing so in the case of his novel; he would say this much, however, like it who would: there was no hope at all for the language if it funked the hard realities of the here and the now, it would become a dead language embalmed in its stilted forms. Could they imagine *The Carpetbaggers* – or even a modern novel of literary merit – in Latin, rich and all a language as it was? It was precisely because he had faith in the future of Irish that he wrote about the smart set with their white Mercs and their villas in Killiney, the sort of people who went skiing in St Moritz or sunbathing in the Bahamas. They too were Irish, whether we liked it or not, every bit as much as the toothless old *seanchaí** mumbling folklore by a fireside in Gweedore or Inchigeela, or the migrant Paddies so beloved of Awley Mac Donnell and other practitioners of the harmless art of autobiography.

This peroration was heard with a fair degree of toleration and the meeting might have ended on a reasonably cordial note but that the aged Caitríona, helped by two young men from his native village of Meenalachan in County Donegal, also mounted the platform and addressed the assembly in a voice that quavered with emotion. They could have their Mercedes and their dicky-bows, their holidays abroad and their scandalous goings-on, he said, but that wasn't Gaeldom no matter what language you used to describe it. That was *Galldachas*** out and out and he was damned if *he'd* ever write about it! "You couldn't – you can't – come out of the mud cabin!" the avant garde taunted him, and, choking with fury, Caitríona yelled back: "And you can't enter it!"

*Storyteller. The seanchaí was the living repository of Irish folklore but radio and television have supplanted him as an entertainer in rural Ireland.

**Foreignness. Invariably, however, it refers to things English.

The convention broke up in disorder but a morose-looking individual who had been staring at Schnitzer all evening approached the poet a little later as he sat with Aengus Mac Proinsias in the Arts Club. "Caitríona has written fifty-five novels," he told Schnitzer without any preamble whatever, "but I've written one novel fifty-five times!"

Schnitzer enquired, in that forthright manner he had picked up from the English, why the other had done anything so ridiculous as this; and the morose-looking individual introduced himself.

"I'm the Crested Grebe," he told Schnitzer as though that in itself explained everything. But O'Shea had never heard of the Crested Grebe up to now and his response was clearly less than the latter expected. "My fame hasn't travelled far," he added sadly and sat down without being asked. The search for perfection was what had made him write his novel over and over again, he told Schnitzer while Aengus Mac Proinsias frowned at the intrusion; each draft of his work, it seemed to him, could be improved upon and no matter how many drafts he wrote he could still see ways of making the thing better. He would give anything to be able to stop this rewriting and submit a final draft to the publishers but it never seemed to him to be good enough for that and he was beginning to wonder if he would ever see his novel in book form.

It was at this juncture that Mac Proinsias, with a raised eyebrow and a discreet sign to the club steward, had the Crested Grebe removed and in some exasperation he explained to Schnitzer what lay behind the Crested Grebe's endless revision of his work. The Crested Grebe had in fact published a novel over a quarter of a century ago, an incredibly rubbishy thing called *The Fraughan* Gatherers about which not even the most lenient of critics could find a good word to say. *The Fraughan Gatherers* was savaged and slated with such ferocity that its author developed a deep and seemingly incurable neurosis about his work and he quite probably was not exaggerating at all when he claimed to have written fifty-five drafts of his second novel. For years the Crested Grebe had pestered everyone he knew, Aengus said, begging them to compare each new draft of his work with the preceeding one until in the

*Bilberry or whortleberry.

end he became such a nuisance that nobody would tolerate him at all. The Crested Grebe had become a pariah, Mac Phroinsias said, and was likely to remain so until he copped himself on.

But the poet was appalled at this, it seemed to him to be the most monumental folly that anyone could be guilty of, an occupation comparable in its futility with that of the legendary Sysiphus who spent all his time rolling a large stone up a steep hill only to have it come tumbling down again; and there and then O'Shea conceived for the unfortunate author of *The Fraughan Gatherers* a mixture of loathing and dread such as a healthy man might feel towards a wretched leper.

"The hoor must be mad," he opined, lapsing into the vernacular of his native Glenbeg and Mac Proinsias agreed that the possibility could not be ruled out. Aengus Mac Proinsias then went on to discuss a programme which he intended making and which he wanted the poet to take part in, but Schnitzer seemed unable to rid his mind of the Crested Grebe and his compulsion to re-write his novel over and over again; as the poet's gloom increased so did the pile of broken matchsticks in the ashtray before him and Mac Proinsias found that he might as well have been speaking to himself for all the interest that Schnitzer was taking.

It was that same night that the poet had the first of a series of nightmares that were to make his sleeping hours a hell and be the cause of him leaving Mrs Fitzgerald's house in Harcourt Villas. Each of these dreams concerned the Crested Grebe and his unending revision, and their effect on the poet was so horrific that he would wake in a lather of cold sweat, jabbering incoherently, the sheets and blankets in a tangled mass about his head. Of course it was only to be expected that the dreadful experience of falling down the lift shaft would have some unpleasant aftermath, psychologically speaking, and Rónán Mac Rónáin has compared Schnitzer's mental state around this time to that of an overloaded electric grid trying to cope with more than it could bear; but more than anything else it was the thought of the morose-featured Crested Grebe forever re-writing his novel that brought O'Shea to the brink.

In one particularly distressing dream Schnitzer saw the Crested Grebe knee-deep in discarded sheets of manuscript, scribbling frenetically and rejecting what he had written almost before the ink itself was dry; the poet woke in a state of considerable agitation, imagining that his room-mate, a junior clerk in the Department of Agriculture not long up from his native Tipperary, was none other than the Crested Grebe. Still under the influence of his nightmare the poet sprang out of bed, clad only in his shirt, and shaking the sleeping clerk he begged him to desist from rewriting his book. The young Tipperaryman sat up in alarm, imagining perhaps that the house was on fire, and demanded to know what was wrong.

"Why do you do it?" Schnitzer enquired. "What's the earthly use of writing the curse-of-God thing over and over again? Does a bricklayer build a wall a dozen times over? Or a painter put on twenty coats of paint?"

In greater alarm now the young clerk begged Schnitzer to tell him what he was on about and Schnitzer replied that he was talking about his novel, the rubbishy novel he was forever rewriting: did he not think it was time to pack it in, or what kind of a lunatic was he at all, at all? The stricken youth protested that he had never read a novel in his life, let alone try to write one; in truth, he declared, it took him all his time to write home once a week, so why would he try to write a novel? But still in the grip of his nightmare the poet was infuriated at this denial and, dragging the terrified young man from between the warm sheets, he challenged him to deny that he was the bane of his fellow writers in Dublin, pestering them mercilessly with his worthless scribbling and all his old guff about structure and form. Could he deny that decent people couldn't have a drink in peace without him descending on them with his thrashy fresh drafts?

Distraught, the young civil servant protested that he never entered a public house, that he had the "pin" and that he hoped to keep it, but this only served to infuriate O'Shea all the more.

"Liar!" he accused and began trouncing the clerk who was bleating piteously now, blubbering like a child as he begged to be allowed to return to the warmth of his bed. "Why can't you own up like a man?"

It was then that the young Tipperary man realised that he would do better to assume the role so unjustly apportioned him and with a convincing show of contrition he vowed that he'd never write another line of his novel again, not so much as a

114

comma would be put on paper any more!

"Good man yourself," Schnitzer said, releasing him, and then, with unnecessary cruelty, perhaps, he added that since *The Fraughan Gatherers* had been such a dismal flop there was no reason to imagine that the present effort would be any better however often he rewrote it. "Get yourself a proper job, Grebe, there's bags of work beyond in England," he advised, and, crawling thankfully back into his bed the ashen-faced junior clerk promised most fervently that he would.

The commotion did not pass unnoticed, of course, and next morning when Schnitzer went down to his breakfast he was told by a frosty-voiced Mrs Fitzgerald that he had better find himself other accommodation forthwith. The young clerk had already left, vowing that nothing in the world would induce him to remain there another night.

Chapter Ten.

SCHNITZER'S LIFE COULD now be likened to a rudderless boat that drifts hither and thither at the whim of wind and current with no destination and no purpose. On leaving Harcourt Villas he rented a dingy little room in a squalid tenement with the incongruous address of Belgrave Mansions; unshaven, unkempt and – why deny it? – downright dirty he became something of a recluse almost overnight, no longer frequenting the haunts of the literati, nor even accepting any work on radio or television. His days were spent now in long and pointless itineraries and when he drank at all it was in some grubby little backstreet pub patronized by the poorer classes. There can be little doubt that what the poet craved more than anything else was time for serious reflection, the opportunity to examine at leisure the many exciting new ideas that clamoured in his mind and which the marathon conversations in the pubs had hindered from developing. Nature has its own way of restoring equilibrium and when the poet sat in some out-of-the-way pub now, lingering over his pint of Guinness, his mind was busy with concepts and theories which the casual observer would never have guessed at.

For the most part he held aloof from the other customers though on occasion, when a fresh idea presented itself to him with sufficient urgency, he was unable to keep from discussing it with whoever might be nearest to hand. Once he upset a market woman by asking her if she did not think that linguistic purity was a fallacy since it would seem, even on a cursory examination, that every language was but a corruption of some earlier one. The good woman could not even begin to understand the nature of Schnitzer's question but the reference to purity and corruption outraged her and she unleashed a stream of rich Liffeyside invective to the poet: how dare he insult a respectable widow with improper suggestions and he a Culchiemock* too! Her dear departed would rise in wrath from

* Coillte Maghach, or Kiltimagh in the English form, a town and district in Co Mayo, but on a Dubliner's lips a common term of contempt for a countryman. This is resented by the people of Kiltimagh, a progressive and lively town.

his grave, she declared, drawing her black shawl about her tightly as if to avoid contamination, if he could hear her being spoken to like this by a country mug. Or what was the world coming to at all when a decent woman couldn't have a glass of stout for the good of her health without being propositioned!

The market lady's outcry brought some hostile glances in the poet's direction and wisely, perhaps, he drank up his pint and left; he was less fortunate on another occasion when he rather imprudently asked a drunk docker if he would not agree, on balance, that the state of non-existence (if non-existence could be accurately described as a state) was not preferable to that of existence. The docker was more disposed towards vulgar brawling than philosophical speculation, however, and before they had even begun to explore that avenue of thought properly he lost patience and struck out wildly at Schnitzer. Being sober the poet had not much trouble in avoiding the blow and, bidding the docker good-day, he walked off to resume his meditation in more congenial surroundings.

But all of this – his shabby appearance, his daily peregrinations, the abrupt severing of his connection with the literary world – gave the rumour-mongers plenty of ammunition and they fabricated rumours about him as shamelessly as they had done about the Crested Grebe in the past. Schnitzer, it was said, had been seen up at the Zoological Gardens in the Phoenix Park, staring ruminatively at the monkeys, or loitering by the edge of the duck pond where he had harangued the various species of wildfowl in ringing tones; he had been seen, so they said, hanging about the entrance of the Gresham Hotel importuning wealthy tourists with questions that alarmed or annoyed them, and he had been seen, too, on the pier in Dún Laoghaire gazing disconsolately out to sea. Yet others claimed that he spent long hours in the *Busáras** studying the timetables, and that he had to be forcibly ejected from the Office of Weights & Measures where he sought to expose the officials' ignorance of their own bye-laws by quoting the opaquely-worded ordinances chapter and verse.

O'Shea would not have grudged the fabricators their bit of fun which was only verbal after all, but one day he met Pacelli

---

* *Bus station, literally bus building.*

O'Mahoney on Aston Quay and on his return to Britain O'Mahoney wrote a quite scurrilous piece about him in *Trowel & Templet,* the organ of the Allied Builders Union. Pacelli had come to Dublin as a fraternal delegate from the ABU to attend an educational conference in Liberty Hall, the headquarters of the Irish Transport & General Workers Union, and as he had not been to Dublin for some years the union man availed of the opportunity to renew his acquaintance with the city, visiting places of historical interest as well as dropping in for the odd jar to working-class pubs. It was quite by chance that Pacelli came across Schnitzer and he was a little shocked at the shabby picture the poet presented; O'Mahoney, like many Marxists, had a definable streak of the conventional in him.

"Is it yourself?" Pacelli asked, unsure for a moment whether it was the poet or not.

"It is," replied Schnitzer, though one feels he might well have denied it if he could for his last encounter with O'Mahoney had been anything but cordial.

"We look a little seedy, Brother, don't we?" Pacelli offered, condescendingly.

Schnitzer did not feel obliged to comment upon this but Pacelli had no intention of letting up, his mind already busy with the article he would write about his meeting with O'Shea. "I thought we were riding on the crest, Brother," he went on, "I thought we went down big over here?"

Again the poet refused to be drawn but far from deterring O'Mahoney this only sharpened his appetite for a story. "I thought we were living in the proverbial lap, Brother, wining and dining and all that! Babbling on the box, articulating on the air, posing in the Press, eh? I thought we were the greatest discovery since the safety pin; gifted genius, new voice and all the rest? So what's the score, Brother?"

"I think," Schnitzer said as though emerging from a dream, "that there has to be finitude in spatial terms. The concept of infinitude seems to me to be unsustainable."

"They've dropped you, Brother!" Pacelli exclaimed, switching to the singular and ignoring what Schnitzer had just said. "They always do you know, that's the pattern – first they pick you up and then they let you down. You'd have done better sticking with your own class, Brother O'Shea: there's

119

never any respect for the toady and the turncoat, I could have told you that from the start!"

Schnitzer considered the observation but declined to reply and Pacelli warmed to his theme. "Oh it's happened before," he declared with obvious relish. "*You're* not the first poor slob of a worker to be ditched by the bourgeoisie and the trendies. They tried to make a monkey out of MacGill, too, giving him a job as a reporter – chucking him in at the deep end, so to speak, for the fun of seeing him trying to swim."

O'Mahoney took a breath for a moment and regarded Schnitzer with a blend of pity and distaste. "The difference between you and Pat MacGill, Brother, is that MacGill had dignity."

"Dignity," O'Shea echoed absently, his mind no doubt elsewhere.

"A quality that elevates dustman above duke, Brother."

The Liffey flowed past, uncaring, and O'Mahoney who had a more genial side to his nature however rarely he might display it suggested they have a drink; once in the pub, however, the ABU delegate began probing again. "So what's the angle then, Brother? What's with the dosser-look, why so unkempt and uncared?"

This was a presumption that Schnitzer ignored with a dignity that should have been apparent to O'Mahoney and they parted before long with no expression of regret on either side. The following week Pacelli's article appeared in *Trowel & Templet* under the heading "Schnitzer O'Shea Pseudo-Bum!" Briefly what the article tried to say was that the poet (referred to throughout as hack, lackey and fraud) had developed a new gimmick in a desperate attempt to get back in the limelight again after being ditched by his media friends. O'Shea was shrewd enough to realise that the carnival of booze and blether couldn't go on indefinitely, that the public had begun to rumble him, so to speak, that he was "kaput!" unless he could find some other wheeze to fool the people. Thus, reasoned Pacelli, O'Shea had resorted to the rakish-genius bit, the drop-out hippy thing, the Kharma Bums lark and Dylan Thomas/Brendan Behan caper all rolled into one: a cunning ploy to gain the kind of notoriety which writers with nothing to say courted. O'Shea was all washed-up, a pathetic has-been, and this was his last frantic bid for attention.

120

There was more in this tedious vein and though it is of scant importance it throws a revealing light on the working of the ABU man's mind. There can be little doubt that O'Mahoney's capacity for honest judgement had been badly warped by years of haggling over pay and conditions, of always attributing motives and machinations to others and of never taking anything on trust. Schnitzer didn't give a tinker's damn what Pacelli or anyone else thought of him but he should not have been pilloried like that, even in so fustian a source as *Trowel & Templet*.

J UST HOW long the poet might have continued in this aimless way of life is impossible to say but as often happens it was an outside agency that was to determine his future. O'Shea's financial situation was dire since he was no longer earning money on radio or television and the royalties from *Milestones* were long overdrawn. Schnitzer did not require much to live on, it is true, but he had become disenchanted with Dublin and he hankered more and more for Northmanton and the contentment he had known there. Mother Perkins, for all her odd ways, was the best friend he ever had and as he trudged about the damp streets of the Irish capital it was only natural that he should think with longing of their little sessions in the Hope & Glory and yearn to be back there again. And so, when he received an offer to appear on a special edition of Gabe Urney's *Late Lately Show*, the poet accepted: it meant a ticket back to Northmanton and a perhaps saner way of life.

The proposed *Late Lately Show* was quite explosive in its choice of subject: a confrontation between the various bodies that made up the Gaelic Revival Movement and the LFM; and the impressario, Gabe Urney, was determined to make it the kind of pyrotechnical success which he knew it could be. A battery of antagonists was assembled for the great debate and it was to Cathal Pádraig Ó Grianáin, flown over specially from Britain, that the task of winkling Schnitzer out of Belgrave Mansions fell and of persuading him to appear on the show; a task the Ulsterman accomplished with his customary zeal. When Ó Grianáin turned up at Montrose for the programme he had Schnitzer in tow, not immaculately dressed it may be, but more presentable than anyone had seen him for several months before.

The programme kicked off in sparkling form with Gabe Urney laying it on the line (as he phrased it) for the studio audience and viewers at home. They had here tonight two conflicting opinions, the seemingly irreconcilable views of those who wanted to drop the Irish language altogether and those who believed that it must be preserved and restored at all costs. His own position, Gabe Urney explained, was that he had no linguistic hang-ups one way or the other: he spoke English because it was the language that he knew best and it was also – barring he was much mistaken! – the language of near-as-damn-it everyone he met in the course of the day. On the other hand he had nothing at all against Irish and if the people of Ireland should take it into their heads to revert overnight to their ancestral tongue then he'd gladly tag along with them. Language was about communication, after all, and you couldn't hope to retain the popularity of a programme like the Late Lately Show if you presented it in a language that the vast majority of the viewers didn't understand. One had to take cognizance of reality and if the people of Ireland were really serious about their first official language and wished to bring it back, then for goodness sake let them get out the text-books and spend their annual holidays in Carraroe or Ballyvourney or wherever they sprachen ze Gaelic, and quit bellyaching about Oliver Cromwell and Poyning's Law*: that was all just an excuse for our own failure to bring about those national aims we were forever proclaiming!

When the applause that followed Gabe Urney's address had died down a newly-formed pop group (a bizarrely garbed trio of indeterminate gender) sang a song called "Shed the shackles of the past"** and the debate got under way, a debate that was

* Fourteenth century legislation enacted by England to halt the Gaelicization of the Anglo-Norman settlers who were fast becoming "More Irish than the Irish themselves". Among other provisions of this very severe law the "mere Irish" were forbidden to "strut and swagger" on the streets of the English towns and within the Pale.

** Shed the shackles of the past
   Give us monoling at last!
   Ditch those ancient, hairy words
   Gaelic's strictly for the birds!
This group, Freedom Freaks, were generally believed to have been the creation of

122

to prove the most acrimonious of any that ever took place on Irish television with insults and charges being hurtled to and fro in the most appalling manner. Ms Shona O'Ryan, the leader of the Language Freedom Movement was accused of wanting to commit cultural genocide by Rónán Mac Rónáin and she accused him of naked fascism.

"The lady is well qualified to talk about fascism," Mac Rónáin taunted and Ms O'Ryan replied that she didn't need to possess a degree in political science to tell a fascist when she saw one. At this Aengus Mac Proinsias, smiling blandly, suggested that Shona O'Ryan would have been an invaluable aide to the late unlamented Joe McCarthy and unabashed Ms O'Ryan agreed that perhaps she would; she had a sharp nose for commies, too! Then Cathal Ó Grianáin, eyes flashing behind his old-fashioned spectacles like the beacon on a squad-car, attacked the LFM in the most intemperate language, calling them a bunch of renegades and national apostates, unworthy of being called Irish. In reply Shona O'Ryan likened Ó Grianáin and his supporters to a bunch of jack-booted Nazis, trampling undemocratically over the Irish people in a vain effort to force an archaic and useless language down their unwilling throats (the metaphors might have been badly mixed but there was no mistaking the sincerity in her voice!) What did it matter what language people spoke as long as they understood each other, she asked, was not communication the purpose of language, as Gabe had suggested, and if you were in the habit of calling a motor-car a motor-car why get your tongue in a twist attempting to call it a "gloosthawn"? This deliberate mispronunciation of the delicately vowled *gluaisteán* brought howls of annoyance from the Revivalists and, revelling in their anger, Ms O'Ryan spat out a list of similar mispronunciations, pejorative expressions like "amadhaun" and "bosthoon" and "ownshuck"*. Rising from his seat in a fury Cathal Ó Grianáin yelled at the leader of the LFM that the adulterous King Henry the Eighth and his daughter Good Queen Bess must be delirious with joy to hear

Shona O'Ryan to whom the words of the song are also credited. Both the LFM and the Freaks are long moribund and the ditty never caught on.

* Óinseach, *a woman fool*; amadán (*amadhaun*) *refers to the male of the species.*

123

the bearer of a noble Irish name advocating the work which they had begun with such enthusiasm back in the sixteenth century, the destruction of our ancient tongue and the transformation of Éire into another England. Why not go the whole hog, Ó Grianáin demanded, and along with consigning our native tongue to the flames of obscurity* re-name all our towns and cities after places in England?

To all this Ms O'Ryan replied that "Mr Grennan" should remember on which side his bread was buttered and show a little gratitude. He had gone to Britain to earn his living and this was a poor way of repaying the debt! But there was no debt and no call for gratitude, Ó Grianáin came back: he had given up a good career here in Ireland to follow our exiles abroad and do what he could to promote the welfare of the language. He was pro-Irish, not anti-English, the Ulsterman declared; every country should uphold its cultural heritage and he was all for the retention of things that were truly English – in England – things like Morris Dancing and other old customs. He had even taken part in a Morris Dance at a folk festival in Berkshire recently Cathal Ó Grianáin claimed and this statement provided one of the few light moments of the evening, the studio audience erupting into a sudden roar of laughter and Shona O'Ryan nipping smartly in to observe that the author of *Mein Kampf* had also been a keen supporter of folk-dancing!

At this stage Gabe Urney threw the discussion open to the studio audience and a woman who described herself as a Gaeltacht** mother of ten spoke up to say that she would like to take this opportunity of condemning the government for its niggardly treatment of the people of the Gaeltacht, the people who still preserved the ancient tongue of the Gael as their everyday speech. What use was the miserly grant of ten pounds per child per annum in these inflationary times, was not the preservation of our national language worth ten times that much? Or for how long did the government expect the people of the Gaeltacht to bear the burden of speaking Irish with no financial recognition worth mentioning? If the government gave a damn about Irish they'd increase the grant to a hundred pounds per child at once! Predictably there were

* *A dreadful malapropism accounted for, possibly, by Ó Grianáin's agitated condition.*
** *An area where Irish is the everyday language of the people.*

124

shrieks of "Tax-payers money! The Gaeltacht is bleeding us dry!" from the ranks of the LFM and rather scathingly the Gaeltacht mother of ten told the protesters that if they would reckon up what the personal cost had been to each of them she would gladly recompense them before leaving the studio. It would be a matter of pennies rather than pounds, she surmised, so let them not be afraid to put their hands out!

The debate raged on for a time and then it became apparent that Schnitzer O'Shea, who had been described earlier by the presenter as the star guest, was taking no part at all in the discussion, nor even indeed making any pretence of being interested. But with the adroitness of his profession Gabe Urney brought the debate under control and then, turning to the poet, asked would he agree with the leader of the LFM that language was a mere means of communication and nothing more?

"The lady is dead right," Schnitzer declared without an instant's hesitation to the patent astonishment of Gabe Urney and the unconcealed delight of Ms Shona O'Ryan; Cathal Ó Grianáin groaned audibly and Rónán Mac Rónáin looked grieved.

"I beg your pardon?" Gabe Urney gasped – a little theatrically, to be sure – and glanced back at his studio audience to gauge the effect of the poet's words on them.

"The good woman is perfectly right," O'Shea repeated with conviction. "The prime and indeed only function of language is to communicate just as the function of a spade is to dig or a saw is to cut."

"Good Lord," Gabe Urney exclaimed as though needing a moment to consider the implications of Schnitzer's statement. "So Mr O'Shea – let's just get this straight now for the benefit of everyone, there are many, I'm sure, who will be surprised at what you've just said – in fact what you're saying is that you don't regard Irish as being any more special than any other language. Is that what you're saying?"

"Precisely," said Schnitzer.

"You don't subscribe to the notion that the Irish language enshrines the psyche of our people, that it is the distillation, so to speak, of our very soul?"

"No," replied Schnitzer, "I do not."

Uncharacteristically, Gabe Urney looked at a loss for a

moment but this may have been more apparent than real for he recovered quickly and warmed to the task. "You don't feel that without Irish Ireland would cease to be Ireland?"

"I don't," the poet answered readily, "I don't think it would make a ha'port of difference."

"Astonishing," Gabe Urney declared with a shake of his head but before he could proceed further Schnitzer began to expound his own ideas about language. "Would you not agree," he asked Gabe Urney as though their roles had been suddenly reversed, "that every language is the product of several other languages and that to attribute a special position to a particular one is to ignore that fact? I'm an Irish speaker, for example, but I don't believe I'd be able to converse very well with King Cormac Mac Airt or with Fionn Mac Cumhail if either of them dropped into the studio now."

The *Late Lately* man wasn't about to exchange roles that easily, however, and he dismissed the poet's proposition with a wave of his hand. "Come on now, Mr O'Shea, that's hardly the point! I'm an English speaker but I don't expect I'd understand much of what King Alfred the Great was saying, either, if he showed up on the programme. Would you not agree now that the Irish language is an integral part of our national being in the same way that English is an integral part of the English national being? Would you not, in fact, agree with what Patrick Pearse himself said: that if Irish died Ireland would die?"

"Not necessarily," said the poet, "because a nation – that is allowing that a satisfactory definition of the word 'nation' may be agreed on – has within it the capacity to survive the loss of the language most associated with it and to retain its own essential character."

This, understandably, was greeted with yells of approval from the Language Freedom Movement's supporters and with angry cries of "Judas!" from the less tolerant among the Gaelic lobby.

"Is Eamonn Andrews as Irish as Aengus Mac Proinsias?" asked one member of the audience while another wanted to know if "How Are Things in Gloccomorra?" was a more Irish song than "Fáinne Geal an Lae": the proceedings were threatening to get out of hand but Gabe Urney quelled the uproar with authority. Then he asked Schnitzer the question that so many others had asked vainly before.

"Very good, then, Mr O'Shea, we can take it that you are not an ardent revivalist, that in fact you would seem to belong as much in the ranks of the LFM as on the other side. Language is no more than a means of communication, it is not the repository of any special virtues or qualities, if I've got you right?" Here the famous interviewer paused to indicate that O'Shea could correct his summation if he wished, but the poet showed no sign of wanting to do so. "Very good then," Gabe Urney went on, "all this begs a most obvious question: why do you write your poetry in Irish when you could, indisputably, reach a far greater number of people by writing in English, the most widely-spoken language in the world?" The silence that followed Gabe Urney's question indicated with what interest the reply was awaited. Schnitzer did not leave them in suspense for long.

"I'm not interested in reaching people," he answered with brutal honesty. "I don't care whether anyone reads my poetry or not: in fact I'd just as soon they didn't!"

The Language Freedom Movement might have been expected to welcome this extraordinary admission as a prop to their case but paranoia never rests. Shona O'Ryan was on her feet at once to comment snidely that no doubt Mr O'Shea knew what he was doing and that if he _had_ written his poetry in English people would be in a position to judge it! Writing in Gaelic* she declared was about as useful an activity as singing roundelays to a bullock.

There was uproar again at this, naturally enough, until Gabe Urney demanded a hearing for Colonel Nigel Hawksforth-Manning (Rtd.), a very fine type of English gentleman who had come to settle in Ireland in disgust with the Labour government's coming to power after World War II. There was too much talk about divisive things in Ireland today, Colonel Hawksforth-Manning said, and he felt they should be concentrating on the things they had in common rather than on the things that divided them. He'd had some splendid southern Irish chaps under his command in the war,

* _LFM members never use the word "Irish" in connection with the Gaelic language – a deliberate ploy to undermine the association between Irish people and their ancestral tongue. Ms O'Ryan's use of "roundelay" betrays her Anglophilic leanings._

127

the Colonel said, and he never heard any of this tiresome twaddle about language from them, they were all united then in the face of the common enemy. Indeed, the Colonel went on, he'd have no objection at all to calling the language which they all spoke "the *British* language": that way the Scots and the Welsh and the Irish could all feel it was their language, too, every bit as much as the English!

The outcry from the Irish language side was prolonged and uproarious with angry cries of "Imperialist!" and "Go back to Bognor Regis!" hurled at the hapless Coloned and counter-cries of "Bogmen!" and "Peasants!" coming from the opposition.

Throughout all this furore Schnitzer maintained an air of serene disinterest until, in something akin to desperation, Gabe Urney asked him if he thought there was any merit in Colonel Hawksforth-Manning's idea; thus it was that the poet, recalled from whatever area of meditation he had been absorbed in, turned full face to the camera and recited an entire quad-rifarious alphabetagam as follows:

Author, aura, arid, aught! Bondage, basic, basic, birth! Concept, conflict, calyx, cant! Dazzle, debut, daunting, don! Earthy, earnest, erstwhile, ell! Febrile, fulgent, fabric, fraught! Genius, gothic, garbled, gaunt! Hostile, haven, hamstrung, hunt! Irate, ikon, insect, irk! Judgement, jovial, jansen, Joyce! Ketcher, kosher, kernel, ken! Lucid, lambent, lustrous, lent! Morbid, murky, mores, mold! Novel, nexus, nadir, nub! Occult, object, opus, orb! Pungent, pathos, poignant, pun! Quadrant, quasi, quorum, quote! Rabid, racy, ribald, realm! Surreal, sentient, subject, sunk! Tribal, totem, total, tone! Ullage, ultra, urgent, urn! Valid, venal, vaunted, vain! Waxing, waning, woeful, womb! Xiphias, xiphoid, xyris, xanth! Yokel, yellow, yeoman, yeast! Zealous, zenith, zero, zest!

This was about the extent of Schnitzer's contribution to the programme and Gabe Urney can hardly be blamed for turning to the audience and asking if they thought that "the man was for real"; a question to which the audience replied with a generous affirmative! But after the show, instead of joining the other participants in the hospitality room, the poet slipped quietly away and walked the seven or more miles back to his squalid lodgings in Belgrave Mansions.

A couple of days later, on receipt of his handsome *Late Lately Show* fee, he left Dún Laoghaire on the night boat for Britain.

❧❧❧ Chapter Eleven. ❧❧❧

THINGS HAD ALTERED somewhat in Northmanton during Schnitzer's absence. The town had at last succumbed to the mania for expansion which had attacked so many comely English boroughs with such disastrous results and now multi-storied car parks and concrete flyovers were vying with new shopping precincts and other architectural eyesores to destroy the Northmanton which the poet had known and loved. Jobs were as plentiful in the construction industry now as the ruffianly Connachtmen aboard the old *Princess Maude* had once made them out to be and a posh new St Bridget's Club was even under construction to cater for the numerous arrivals from Ireland, attracted by the boom in work. Accommodation had become correspondingly difficult to find and Mother Perkins' establishment was now chock-a-block as she put it; so full, in fact, that some of the beds which formerly held two now held three (an uncomfortable arrangement to say the least and one which finally brought Lavinia to the attention of the authorities). Schnitzer was now obliged to share his old bed not just with Ginger McGinn – who was happily working a fourteen-hour day and would have slept soundly on the proverbial harrow – but also with a newcomer to the town, none other than Awley MacDonnell of whom more in a moment.

It need scarcely be said that Lavinia was delighted to see Schnitzer again, however well she might have concealed her delight under a testy exterior.

"Strewth, boy – I thought you'd gone to bleedin' Aussieland, I did! What kept you so long, then? You was only supposed to be going for a couple of days and you bin gone over two years by my reckoning!"

"The hens' journey to Scotland,* Mother," Schnitzer told

---

* *According to an old Irish folk-tale the hens in their coop plan nightly to go to Scotland next day but due to their propensity for dallying around the farmyard they never get started on their journey and each night the silly resolution is made all over again.*

her cryptically and though Lavinia did not understand the reference she was content to let it pass. "Well I think this calls for a celebration, Patrick," she declared and they set off for the Hope & Glory across the way. Mother Perkins was now employing a domestic help, an overweight young woman of such scant allure that her virtue was rarely threatened by even the most love-starved among the lodgers.

Lavinia Perkins, too, had changed somewhat in the interval since she and the poet had last sat together in the Hope & Glory; she had become rather subdued by comparison with her old self, at least until she'd put away a few milk stouts and a drop of something stronger. The landing of the first human beings on the moon, while not actually destroying her belief in the Deity had almost brought her to the point of questioning the soundness of His judgement in permitting the Americans to set foot there. Worse still, it gave ammunition to Gladys Webb who crowed over it shamelessly, extolling the resourcefulness of the Yanks and citing their marvellous achievement as proof of her husband's perspicacity in foretelling the event. Mother Perkins' world had been badly shaken, in truth, for if something so remote as the moon could be tampered with what guarantee had we that anything was safe?

"Where's it all going to end, Pat, that's what I'd like to know," she asked gloomily over her first milk stout and the poet replied that the "unknowability" of things was something which he often pondered. He often grew quite depressed, he told Mother Perkins, by the sheer impossibility of knowing all that there was to know.

"I ain't saying we should know everything! A body couldn't just stand knowing everything, the old brainbox would go *whoosh*! just like blowing a fuse! We was never *meant* to know everything, Pat: that's reserved for the Man Above."

"Omniscience," Schnitzer murmured. "Omni-science."

"Call it what you will, Patrick," Mother Perkins said, offering him her snuff-box, "but it all boils down to the same thing; only the dear Lord knows everything, you mark my words!"

The dinner that evening was worse than usual in consequence of Lavinia's absence for so long in the Hope & Glory and some of the lodgers were correspondingly ungracious not only to Lavinia but to Maria, her helper; Schnitzer cleaned his

130

plate thankfully, however, and almost as soon as the meal was over he and the landlady returned to the pub again, leaving the washing-up and the preparation of the sandwiches for the next day to Maria. A body needed a bit of a break, Lavinia said, after the sight of all those miserable bleedin' faces.

In the Hope & Glory Schnitzer and Lavinia resumed their earlier conversation, the landlady reiterating that God saw all and that perhaps he wasn't as soft as some folk seemed to believe. Maybe, she suggested, He had His own ideas in allowing the silly sodding Yanks to land on the moon; giving them enough rope, so to speak, to hang themselves. God wasn't mocked, mate, not bleedin' likely!

Here Schnitzer intervened to question the notion of God being mocked: was it feasible, he asked, to speak of God being mocked; or indeed angered or gratified or anything at all? Did not such supposition, he wondered, seem to impose a human limitation on the Omnipotent in attributing to Him such human emotions as anger or outrage or whatever. Was not God above and beyond mockery, as indifferent to it as a human might be to the feelings of a trodden insect?

"Would you not think that it implies a vulnerability incompatible with the notion of omnipotence?" he asked Lavinia who was perhaps understandably none too pleased at the speculation.

"What you're saying sounds like heathen talk to me, Patrick – blest if it don't boy! I could understand it if you'd been away in some pagan country where they ain't heard the Word yet but the Emerald Isle is a Christian country as everyone knows and I'm blest if I know where you get such ideas! I should trot along and have a word with the Father before it's too late, boy."

Schnitzer did not press the matter but a little later when Bert and Gladys Webb dropped in for a quiet drink Lavinia brought up the moon landing again. It wasn't beyond the powers of modern science to *fake* a landing on the moon, the landlady said, that wouldn't be any trouble at all with all the cameras and thingy-bobs they had nowadays.

"How do we know," she asked aloud, "that the bleedin' Yanks are there at all?"

"Well I'm sure they got ways of proving it," Gladys Webb answered with the assurance of conviction. "We'd have heard

131

before now if it had been a fake, I'm sure we should!"

"Of course there's some as believe everything they hear on telly," Lavinia sneered and Gladys told her sharply that it had been in the papers, too!

"Well, paper won't refuse print," Lavinia retorted, winking at Schnitzer. But Gladys Webb was no longer prepared to let Mother Perkins score points over her and, ostensibly addressing her husband Bert, she said aloud:

"It seems that some folks never give credit where credit's due!"

"Yes," Lavinia answered sweetly, "and it seems that some folks are never done praising the Yanks! But then some folks had quite a lot of truck with the Yanks in their time, hadn't they? Some folks made the Yanks very much at home indeed!"

This quite gratuitous slur on Mrs Webb's reputation proved too much for even the somnolent Bert who responded with a show of spirit that was rare with him. "I say, steady on, Lavinia! That ain't no way to speak, it ain't!"

The guv'nor of the Hope & Glory shared this belief, too, because with no more ado he came out from behind the bar and asked Mother Perkins to leave. "Take old Pat with you, too," he added, "and please don't come back!"

"I shan't, don't you fear!" Lavinia retorted with dignity, then ruined the effect by telling the publican, in the most unladylike language, what he might do with his drink.

"My character's unsullied!" she threw back over her shoulder as the publican ushered Schnitzer and herself out on the street. "There's no skeletons in Lavinia's cupboard!"

The night was early yet and instead of going home – much the wiser course in the circumstances – Mother Perkins insisted that they visit the Navvy's Rest.

"There's more than one sodden pub in this town, Patrick. See if I care!"

But in spite of her valiant protestation Lavinia did care; the humiliation of being thrown out of her own local rankled deeply and the rather depressing atmosphere of the Navvy's Rest did nothing to relieve it. And before they were through with their second drink Lavinia's anger focused on one of the regular patrons there; a shabby-looking fellow who drifted from job to job and never seemed to have a penny. This individual had stayed in Mother Perkins' house for a week and then left without paying any money, indeed without ever bothering to mention that he was going. Whatever Lavinia's other little failings were she was not as grasping as the generality of the landlady sorority and a small show of contrition, of embarrassment even, might have softened her now. But the bilker showed neither contrition nor embarrassment; in fact he gave no sign that he recognised his old landlady at all. Lavinia, understandably, was quite piqued by all this.

"Well, chap – what about it then?" she asked without preamble.

"What about what?" the impecunious one countered, his empty pint glass forlornly before him on the counter.

"The week's money you owe me, chap! I fed you for a bleedin' week and you done a flit, that's what! Right's right and wrong's no man's right," she added, throwing in her favourite maxim.

But the effect of all this was to arouse her ex-lodger from his gloomy contemplation of his empty glass; he too must have had his share of frustrations for he rounded on Mother Perkins now with a scorn that took her quite by surprise.

"Fed, missus? *Fed?* I own to Jasus I often gave more to the oul collie dog back home! Fed?" he repeated, his voice rising dangerously. "There was better feeding in Belsen Camp, so there was! I had a knot in me stomach with hunger the few days I was with you!"

Hardened as she was, Mother Perkins was reduced almost to tears by his blatant display of ingratitude. She retreated, Schnitzer in tow, but there was worse to come on her return home. She stood in the hallway of her house in Balaclava Terrace and announced in a high-pitched wail that she wanted everybody out that instant. Old Patrick was back from Dublin and he wasn't going to see her messed about any more; so would they kindly get their duds together and get out before he chucked them out?

Up to now Mother Perkins' lodgers had endured her histrionics with commendable patience (those of them who didn't actually enjoy the performance) but some of the rougher characters among them did not fancy being threatened with the poet, whose stature in the world of letters impressed them not in the least. That was a challenge to their manly pride and thus it was that as Lavinia advanced up the stairs spitting abuse and contumely, a pugnacious-looking fellow with flattened nose and cauliflowers ears – the product of many a pub brawl – made an appearance on the landing above. Clad only in his singlet and underpants this bruiser glared truculently at Mother Perkins and Schnitzer. She could rant and rave all she liked, he told her – that was her right as landlady – but he wouldn't be threatened by her feckin' side-kick!

"If you fancy your chances, cock, we'll settle it here and now," he offered, switching his attention to Schnitzer. "I'm too long on the road to be worried by a greesheen* like you!"

And nothing loth, the Glenbeg man took him up on it. "Fair enough, mister," he told the bowsie, "I'll take tay with you!"

With the best will in the world one can hardly imagine the poet emerging victorious from a bout of fisticuffs with this unsavoury specimen but fortunately issue was not joined because Mother Perkins, scared almost sober by the prospect of a battle royal, begged the opponents to desist. There was no need at all for that kind of thing, she protested, she wanted her house to be a haven of peace and goodwill, a home from home for her poor dear Irish boys who slogged their guts out all week – as she herself did – for a measly pittance. And then, as an earnest of that same goodwill, she broke into an off-key, quavering verse of "Mother Machree", clinging all the while to Schnitzer either to protect him from his bellicose compatriot on the landing above or in the hope that he could protect her. The unpleasantness blew over in any case when the pugnacious one went back to his bed, grumbling that he wasn't going to be pushed about by anyone. And Schnitzer, after bidding his landlady a very good night, climbed into his own bed along with Ginger McGinn and Awley MacDonnell.

SCHNITZER HAD hoped to take up again the threads of his old life in Northmanton and he might well have settled back to the serenity of his former routine if it had not been for Awley MacDonnell. MacDonnell, a Kilkennyman like Schnitzer, had already achieved some note with his autobiographical writings in Irish and it may be worth examining the

* A word of uncertain origin (but Irish, obviously) meaning "Johnny-come-lately".

phenomenon of the Irish worker-writer before proceeding any further with this narrative. It is rarely indeed that a foundry-man from Port Talbot, a potter from the Black Country or a weaver from Halifax is seized with an irresistible urge to commit his workaday experience of life to paper but the compulsion is fairly common among the Irish, particularly among those who write in the native language, and MacDonnell was just one in a long line of labourers who felt that his story was worth chronicling. Similarly, a great many places in Ireland not distinguished by a very noteworthy claim to scenic beauty have fulsome songs written in their praise while even the most renowned sights in the sister isle are unsung. What English equivalents are there of such songs as "Moonlight in Mayo", the "Old Bog Road", the "Cliffs of Duneen", "Lovely Green Gweedore", "Galway Bay" or a thousand others? Many of these places are justly famed, it is true, but even the most unremarkable places are sung about and mundane events such as a parish football match or a peat-cutting competition may be celebrated in verse. A testament, however venial, to the poetic nature of the Celt?

There was nothing very poetic about the writings of Awley MacDonnell though; in fact they were remarkable for their addiction to the commonplace, the trivial and the banal. Which in a way is surprising because there was a poetical side to Awley's nature as Schnitzer soon found out. At night when the poet wished to sleep or to cogitate on some philosophical concept MacDonnell kept chattering away about home, wallowing in the memories of his youth there and seeking to determine how many acquaintances he and the poet had in common. Had Schnitzer ever been to the Caves of Dunmore and did he know that the treacherous Danes had massacred a peaceful gathering of Irish in the nearby Glens of Kylefarney? Or had he ever compared the clarity of the Irish sky at night with the haziness of that here in Britain? In Ireland, Awley averred, the stars stood out as bright and sharp as diamonds on a black velvet cloak. And what were the things that Schnitzer remembered most about home – the tang of turf-smoke on a frosty night, the swallows flitting above the River Nore in the purple summer dusk, or the smell of new-mown hay?

Worse still, Awley had read *Milestones* many times over and he wanted nothing more than to discuss each and every poem

135

with Schnitzer.

It may be too great an exaggeration to say that Schnitzer developed towards Awley MacDonnell an even greater antipathy than that which he felt for the Crested Grebe but there is no doubt at all that he came to dread the sound of Awley's voice nor that Awley's company was the most unwelcome the poet had ever had to suffer. Schnitzer found himself work on a building contract on the outskirts of Northmanton as soon as his money ran out and there, at least, he should have been free of Awley's prating for eight or nine hours a day; but no, for MacDonnell, with the insensitivity of the true bore, got himself a job on the same site, never imagining for a moment that Schnitzer longed to be free of him. The poet had never been averse to hard work but now he came to dread the daily stint almost as much as he dreaded going to bed at night for either way there was Awley prattling on about home and old times and asking tiresome questions. What language did Schnitzer dream in and if it came to making a choice between English and Irish which language would he relinquish? Did speech come as naturally as movement to the human species and would a colony of infants, left to themselves, evolve a language of their own?

For O'Shea, absorbed in his speculation on the relationship between our perception of material objects and the true nature of these objects themselves, it was tedious in the extreme to have MacDonnell chunter on and on *ad nauseam* about his own footling preoccupations, attaching weight and significance to ideas that the poet would dismiss as banal. How fortunate, Awley would burble, to be born into the twentieth century and not into the servitude of feudal times, or the grim days of the industrial revolution?

"Ah, Schnitzer," he said one day with a share of emotion hardly called for in the circumstances, "think of our poor wretched ancestors living in terrible squalor! Toiling from dawn till dusk for a few coppers with dirt and disease all about them!"

Schnitzer had more weighty things to think about and he did not encourage Awley by word or sign; but Awley went on just the same. "Today, me oul pal, we enjoy a standard of living they never dreamed of," he declared as he struggled, ankle-deep in effluent, to unblock a line of sewer-pipes laid

136

carelessly some time previous to this by a fly-by-night gang of subbies. "If we lived back home a hundred years ago," he continued, "we'd have to exist on a diet of skim-milk and spuds with the landlord and his men at the door of the cottage howling for the rent. And if we lived over here we'd not be much better off: we'd be crammed into some horrible Victorian slum, despised and exploited. No welfare state, no national health, no free milk for the schoolkids! We're in clover, Schnitzer me oul pal, if we only knew it!"

It was typical of Awley that when hearking back to former times he could conceive himself as belonging only to the poorest section of society (unlike Gilbert Keith Chesterton who waxed nostalgic for the baronial halls and the roast ox of "Merry England") and so it is not surprising that he should have been duly appreciative of modern life. Nor would Schnitzer have disputed much of what Awley said, but he did not believe it was something which demanded constant reiteration nor that one should never outgrow the novelty of finding employment so plentiful in England. Naivety may be pardoned in the young but the author of *Navvy's Notebook* was getting a little long in the tooth now. It was unfortunate for the poet that at the very time that he was beginning to recover from the effects of his Dublin sojourn he should have Awley MacDonnell inflicted upon him like this.

But it was MacDonnell's unwavering commitment to his diary, more than anything else, that earned him the loathing with which the poet soon came to regard him. Awley would no more let a day pass without making a full and minute entry in his diary than he would have gone without food; he entered the most ordinary everyday things in his bulging notebook with the same sense of wonder that some intrepid traveller might record his experiences in the most far-flung corner of the earth. The various tasks he performed each day Awley entered in his diary more assiduously than the most bonus-greedy employee filling out a time-sheet. If he unloaded six lorries of bricks in the course of the day, or shovelled ten yards of concrete, MacDonnell wrote it all down together with whatever piffling observations he wished to make on the excellence of modern working conditions; the price of the cup of tea or the bacon sandwich in the site canteen was duly recorded along with the comment that no such amenities were enjoyed in former times, and if he and Schnitzer called into the Navvy's Rest on their way from work Awley would note who was present and what had been said as though the desultory conversation of the Mule Kennedy's men was something to be saved for posterity. To make matters worse Awley filled his diary in bed at night, the nib of his fountain-pen scratching the page like the beak of a demented bird trying to free itself of an obstruction; and it was this practice that finally proved too much for the poet.

"Why don't you pack it up, Mac?" he asked Awley one night above the snores of Ginger McGinn.

"Pack what up?" Awley asked absently, pen rasping on the page of his notebook.

"Your scribbling," Schnitzer said bluntly.

"Scribbling?" Awley echoed, confused. "I'm filling my diary."

"I know what you're doing but I don't know why. What's the point of it, Mac; don't you think it's a waste of good ink?" Schnitzer enquired flatly.

It was also a characteristic of Awley's that he was slow to take offence, indeed that he was very often unaware that he had cause to feel offended. And so, with the air of one settling down to a friendly discussion, he told the poet that he didn't think it a waste of ink at all; on the contrary, he felt that everybody should keep a diary, that each person's life was so unique it was a great pity that everyone could not be compelled to keep a diary. Had Schnitzer ever considered what a wealth of social history had been lost to mankind through the illiteracy of our forefathers?

"Just think," he continued with the enthusiasm of the fanatical, "what a wonderful thing it would be if they discovered a diary left behind by some poor slave who worked on the Egyptian pyramids; or even a navvy who worked on the London to Manchester railway line a hundred years ago!"

The notion did not at first recommend itself very strongly to the poet but it took root, just the same, and he would dwell on it a few years hence in the course of his gargantuan poem-novel, A Cry From the Pits. That night, however, as he listened to the scratching of Awley's pen Schnitzer quietly resolved not to stay in Balaclava Terrace any longer. As with Muldowneyscourt and Dromawn Aneerin in the barony of

Glenbeg there was no going back to the happy life he had known and next day he bade goodbye to Northmanton and a tearful Mother Perkins who begged him to come back sometime, if only for a visit.

✤✤ Chapter Twelve. ✤✤

FROM NORTHMANTON SCHNITZER O'Shea went to London where he found accommodation of a kind that permitted him enough solitude for meditation and for the perfection of his poetic gift without at the same time cutting him off from the society of others. This was in Arlington House in Camden Town, one of the many such charitable institutions set up in the last century by the philanthropic Lord Rowton for the benefit of homeless workingmen, and colloquially reffered to as "the Rowter." Here in the privacy of his tiny cubicle, safe from the vexatious sound of Awley MacDonnell's voice, the poet began to formulate the ideas he would express so memorably in his next collection of verse. Arlington House had many Irishmen among its rather down-at-heel inhabitants, most of whom, like the poet himself, wanted nothing more than to be left alone to plough their lonely furrows or to fade from ken like a ditty of yesteryear; and it was here, among a community which respected a man's wishes for anonymity or accepted without question whatever face it was he wished to present to the world, that Schnitzer grappled with strange new concepts, hewing poetic shape and form from the sometimes amorphous mass of ideas that simmered in his feverish brain.

For Schnitzer his coming to London was a final renunciation of conformity, a cutting loose, so to speak, from the herd. He no longer bothered to seek regular employment but worked the odd casual shift as a kitchen porter or as a labourer on some building site where the lump was in operation and where a man's identity was of no more consequence than his date of birth. Detractors like Pacelli Ignatius O'Mahoney have tried to make out that the poet's spell in Dublin had sapped his will to work; confusing the state of unemployment with that of idleness! But O'Shea was never an idler and even now he expended more energy in the course of a day, quite often, than many a man who congratulates himself on having done a good day's work. He was still a prodigious walker, going sometimes as far as Hendon or Southall in the course of a day while memorizing, *en route*, long lists of street names, terraces, avenues, crescents and squares – scarcely the mark of indolence one must agree.

Camden Town was the hub from which Schnitzer sallied forth on his daily excursions, treks of discovery that took him into out-of-the-way holes and corners, those many little oases of peace and quiet that delight and surprise the visitor to London; and just as delivery-men and taxi-drivers come to have a minute knowledge of the metropolis O'Shea came to know it as few Londoners do. As for the charge of being lazy, whenever he worked a casual shift on a building site or in a cable-gang Schnitzer unfailingly impressed his foreman or ganger with his capacity for hard work . . . again and again he was offered regular employment when others were told not to apply any more!

But in truth the poet's needs were quite few now for in an area where cheap workingmen's cafés abounded he could get what food he required for a few shillings a day, and whenever he worked as a scullion or as a kitchen-hand there were always generous portions of leftovers from the dining-rooms above. As time went on Schnitzer discovered even cheaper means of subsistence in the form of unsaleable foodstuffs, stale bread, damaged fruit or wilting vegetables. The London market folk were generous towards the end of the day and when necessity dictated Schnitzer did not scruple to ask some passerby for the price of a cup of tea, or a jam-sandwich, even. There were those among his compatriots who despised the poet for what they regarded as his descent into beggary but the true artist does many things for the sake of his art and surely the riches that the poet bestows on society compensate for whatever little gratuities he receives. Poets have starved in garrets and great painters gone to bed hungry, and therein lies the test of a true artistic vocation; for who can doubt that scribblers like Awley MacDonnell, however hard-working or prolific, if faced with the choice of pick or pen would not forsake the pen and console themselves with a regular pay-packet?

But Schnitzer did not expend bodily energy only in his long meanderings all over London. The poet's appetite for knowledge was quite insatiable now and he would spend long hours in the public libraries of the various boroughs perusing great tomes of such diverse and arcane nature as *The Theory* and Practice of Aerodynamics or Palaeontological Relics of Central America not to mention a wide range of philosophical and metaphysical studies. Craving to sample every branch of learning Schnitzer was now akin to the busy bee for whom the hours of daylight are never long enough, as he dipped into hundreds of scholarly works, greedily absorbing their treasures. O'Shea was driven by a burning urgency, it was as though he feared that his lifespan would end before he could amass the great wealth of knowledge that towered like the Matterhorn above him. Midas-like O'Shea now coveted more knowledge than any man could hope to possess, and the power of this terrible yearning cries out poignantly in poems like "The Midas Touch" (*Doulton Glaze* p 43):

> To crave the magic Midas touch
> whose univalence conquers all
> or Finn's* sage thumb that opens wide
> the gaping depths of Wisdom's maw;
> to yearn for Learning's priceless store
> with pike-like hunger unassuaged,
> to covet Arry's** precious hoard
> of jewelled knowledge, page by page . . .

Such was Schnitzer's dream now, unattainable as he must have known it to be, and how ironic that those whose vision ranged no farther than the securing of a mortgage or a pensionable job should presume to despise one whose mental horizons, for all the inadequacy of his education, compared with their own as the South American pampas compare with the little patch of green in Euston Square. Yet there were many such, some of them as intolerant of the poet as they were ignorant of his poetry.

Not content with his study sessions in the reading rooms of public libraries Schnitzer spent his weekends at Speakers' Corner where he would go from platform to platform listening attentively to what was being said and sometimes debating with the speaker, joining with particular relish in the meta-

---

* *Fionn McCool, properly Fionn Mac Cumhail, the legendary Irish hero and the possessor of the Thumb of Knowledge which he had but to suck to learn whatever he wanted to know.*

** *Colloquial Irish for Aristotle, often referred to in Gaelic folklore. O'Shea would have heard of Arry from his grandfather in Glenbeg.*

physical and philosophical discussion that so often raged but taking no part at all in the political arguments. Politics never appealed to O'Shea and the political views expressed in the park interested him only as an illumination of the human mind, "the troubled forum of blinkered thought" was how he described political debate in his "Spring in Marble Arch" (*Doulton Glaze* p 96) and his republican compatriots were long angered at his failure to support their cause. The fact is, of course, that Schnitzer was incapable of thinking along merely political lines and he genuinely could not see that it mattered a jot who ruled whom. It may be irrefutable that O'Shea never wrote a line or uttered a word in condemnation of British rule in Ireland but he would have remained just as unmoved had the position been reversed and Ireland ruled a sizeable chunk of Britain. Schnitzer's view of such matters was truly Olympian: human beings are human beings, he would have said, irrespective of political allegiances, and not so very different to a colony of scurrying ants preoccupied with their pathetic little chores!

Betjeman and other poets have written about the lure of Speakers' Corner, but it is doubtful if any poet, in any language, has captured the feel of the place as O'Shea did in "Spring in Marble Arch":

They're washing dishes now
deep in the
bowels of
the Cumberland
Hotel
in Marble Arch.
Rattle of delph and crockery,
the silver shoal of cutlery
rings hollow and
sad . . .
Steam and echo oppress the pallid
drudge —
Unclocked cards may lead to loss of pay!
But high above
beneath the
canyon's rim
of Oxford Street the valiant daffodil
tossing
a festive head, proclaims

it's Spring!
Likewise the clamourous crows
home-making
in the greening
trees above the
fluxing throng
that swells and breaks again like tides
in thrall to Luna's
pull –
a timeless spell.
The power
of orator and
demagogue
that thrills
the troubled forum of blinkered thought
(who'd die for a
flag – say, rag!)
provoking discord
too . . .
What harm!
The crows are building
still
and men are drinking pints
of mild
in the New Inn on
Edgeware Road.

Schnitzer knew all about the steam and echoes of the
Cumberland for he had often worked there for a day or two at a
time washing delph and cutlery; though as his appearance
grew progressively more Bohemian even that kind of menial
employment was refused him. Not that he minded at all for his
needs were growing steadily fewer until in the end he could get
by all day on a bowl of soup and a crust of bread. There is an
account in Awley MacDonnell's *Leaves From a Labourer's
Diary* of his meeting with the poet in Speakers' Corner and it
may not come amiss to give a short extract here though in
truth it tells us more about Awley's irritating simplicity than it
does about O'Shea.

"Walked from Euston station to Camden Town where I had
a tasty meal (pork chop, chips, tea and bread and butter) for
four and six. Drank a pint of Watney's in the Dublin Castle
and there met an old Irishman who has not been home for

forty years, said he hates every stone in London. Underground to Marble Arch and Speakers' Corner to savour the cut and thrust of debate, the sparkling wit and repartee; reflected on the wonderful liberty the people of Britain enjoy where the public speakers may say what they will, 'Down with the Monarch' or 'Out with the Government' with no fear of the midnight knock. In the park there were communists advocating the overthrow of the system, Irish republicans demanding the return of the Six Counties, atheists denying the existence of God and one old African with a black homburgh and a bad facial twitch prophesying that the black man will rule the world. How invigorating it all is and how magnanimous the country that permits it! Prince Monolulu was resplendent in his robes and ostrich plumes selling racing tips and crying 'I gotta hoss' and McGuinness, the Dubliner, was there on his perch telling the English that they'd lost their dynamism, that he preferred them when they went all over the globe with the Bible in one hand and the sword in the other kicking the damned natives into line and showing them who was the boss!

But then, a most pleasant surprise: bumped into Schnitzer O'Shea listening to a debate on existentialism! Did not grasp all the points under debate myself but overjoyed of course to meet Schnitzer again. The poet has grown a luxuriant beard and his appearance could be described as ragged; still manners maketh the man, not the clothing. I prevailed on him to adjourn for a jar to the Green Man in Edgeware Road and gave him all the news of Northmanton on the way; he spoke very little, though, and he had no more than sampled his pint when he excused himself to visit the gents – and that was the last I saw of him whatever befell him at all."

One hardly blames Schnitzer for giving Awley the slip but the significance of their meeting is that back in Northmanton Awley lost no time in reporting to Cathal Ó Grianáin that the poet frequented Speakers' Corner; and Ó Grianáin, notwithstanding that he was still a little annoyed with Schnitzer because of his behaviour on the *Late Lately Show*, turned up the following weekend in Marble Arch. There he located the poet and persuaded him to hand over the sizeable batch of poems he had written since returning to Britain. Thus, once again, it was the Ulsterman who was responsible for ensuring the publication of O'Shea's work, his second collection, *Doulton Glaze*, and all his subsequent composition.

D OULTON GLAZE met with a far more mixed reception than *Milestones*. That the poet had matured greatly or that his breadth of vision had widened is beyond doubt but there were those among his public who did not welcome his development at all, who would have him remain immobile as a butterfly pinned in a showcase, tread endlessly the same old paths, or rake vainly over the ashes of dead inspiration. But the cosy familiarities of *Milestones* were behind him now and he was committed to the deeper waters of experimentation and innovation. Those who understood the poet's need for fresh modes of expression hailed his maturing talent and saw in it a promise of still greater things to come while those who could not stomach his bleaker vision of life withdrew shivering like a petulant matron who complains that the sea is too cold to bathe in. "Doulton Glaze", the title poem of the second collection, aroused the ire of the unadventurous but discerning critics were quick to give the poem its due. That "Doulton Glaze" represents a big advance in technique upon anything he had written before is obvious and Vidor T. Whitmere refers to the "onomatopaeic precision" of the work; "Doulton Glaze", in the biographer's opinion, begs comparison with the best of contemporary European verse:

Below the busy highway's
drowsy drone
hushed, muted like a slumbering
summer
sea
in geometric stasis,
this quiet
oasis,
retreat of sweet serenity
where echoing
footfalls pass
like ghostly sounds . . .
Where each cool slab
of
Ancient glaze,

cross-veined
with
minute fissures webbed intricately
a cartographer's dream of some
far world
conceived within the questing mind of
man . . .
A glacial cliff new-cleansed with every flow
that gushes,
gurgling,
from the groaning duct,
the winged urinals stand, a serried row,
emblazoned with
their ancient heraldry
of *Doulton Glaze.*
And high above, beside the rusting vent
the glass-faced cistern frets
by some decree
a puny ocean caged for all to see
and
drips
drop –
drip-drop!
drop-drip!
drip-drip-drop!
drop-drop-drip!
in tuneless
threnody.
The coughing man-in-charge with tinkling keys
and fag-end stuck to blue, bronchitic lips,
gains strength to shine the gleaming
rail –
brave brass that restitutes the errant beam
of golden sunlight as the open lake
reflects the azure sky . . .
Heark! the swift rush, a mountain stream
undammed and leaping
free –
the cistern's reservoir, a cataract
in miniature . . .
whole worlds are drowned in its immensity
for as our pygmy planet to some stars
is but a speck – at most a shrivelled pea –
so worlds so miniscule exist, a flea

148

might span them like Collossus!
Hiroshimas happen
in
some small universe
with every
sneeze.

Doulton Glaze was a giant step forward and O'Shea could not have progressed from the assumptions and certainties of *Milestones* to his greater, later work without having first of all passed through that stage of maturation which gave us *Doulton Glaze*. But the poet himself was blithely unaware of the fuss and furore created in Dublin by his second book of poetry; he did not even bother to read the many reviews which Cathal Ó Grianáin so carefully cut out and posted to him in Arlington House. And if he had read them Schnitzer would have been equally unmoved by the comment which appeared in *The Furrow* – "Drunken maundering more appropriate to the walls of the edifice that inspired it!" – and by Vidor T. Whitmere's perceptive observation that *Doulton Glaze* was a valiant attempt to find in the very ugliness of life that same beauty that reposes in a flower, a dawn or a sunset. O'Shea would not have cared a rotten straw what anybody said or thought; his poetry, as far as Schnitzer O'Shea was concerned, was the urgent expression of the ideas that bubbled within him, thoughts and ideas to be examined and resolved within the ambit of his own being, and thus (as he saw it) entirely unrelated to others. Iconoclastic, perhaps, but the poet could no more take note of the controversy that raged around his work than Sophocles, sunk deep in meditation, would be distracted by the squabbling of children.

But controversy is a good salesman and though Schnitzer's earnings from *Doulton Glaze* may have been modest enough by the standards of successful prose writers they were more than sufficient to maintain his frugal living until the publication of his third collection, *Who Is Humphrey Deegan?* a year later. O'Shea was free to spend as long as he wished over his studies now, immersing himself in the writings of Kant and Hegel, Descartes, Leibniz and others, working his way through their enormous wealth of thought like some solitary diamond-miner eating into the bowels of a mountain. When Schnitzer left the Rowton house in an effort to shun the publicity which his stature as poet was bringing him, the walls of his little cubicle were scribbled over with maxims and aphorisms:

Experience is no substitute for thought. A cow experiences . . . Matter exists independently of how it may be perceived to exist . . . When a thing has once been it could not not have been; that which is will have been and the future can not but become the present . . . Belief begets disbelief.

These and many other nuggets of wisdom or speculation gave the poet food for thought through many a lonely night and they would all have their place like some vast mosaic of Byzantine intricacy in the epic work that was already gestating within him.

❧❧ Chapter Thirteen. ❧❧

DREAMS HAVE ENGAGED the speculation of philosophers from earliest times and they have, on occasion, inspired works of art. One night while still tenanting his cubicle in Arlington House, Schnitzer had an unusual dream. He was back in Northmanton again and working in the Mule Kennedy's gang; the gang was busily excavating a cable-trench and Schnitzer was teamed up with young Owenie Garrigan as he had been so often in reality. In Schnitzer's dream Owenie Garrigan leant on the handle of his shovel for a moment and, pointing to his bruised and blackened eye, said quite dispassionately, and without the slightest trace of a stammer, "Humphrey Deegan gave me that".

This was the extent of Schnitzer's dream for he woke at that moment, but it intrigued and fascinated him as no other dream had ever done. Schnitzer had an excellent memory and he would have remembered the name of Humphrey Deegan if he had ever heard it before, but he had not and of that he was certain. The poet had known one or two Deegans (the surname is not uncommon) and if he had not actually met anyone called Humphrey he had at least heard the name; but he had never, in all his life, heard or even seen these two names in conjunction. Was there any such person as Humphrey Deegan? the poet asked himself as he lay in his narrow bed staring into the darkness, or by what odd process of selection did the sleeping mind place together so improbable a combination of names? And, having done so, why put them in the mouth of so unlikely an oracle as Owenie Garrigan? Was there some message here, some hidden portent? Had some unexplored region of the subconscious furnished him with data, computer-like, to help the conscious mind unravel the mysteries that engaged it?

Schnitzer puzzled over his strange dream for the rest of the night; and in the months that followed he ransacked the works of Freud and Jung in a vain search for some clue, some illumination of the riddle. O'Shea could accept that the overcoming of one's inner resistance to an understanding of self was a prerequisite to understanding a dream, but he could not go along with Freud's assertion that there was no such thing as the arbitrary determination of the mind; the evidence, in Schnitzer's opinion, pointed to the contrary. Jung was no more helpful, nor any of the other sources the poet turned to for enlightenment, and thus he was thrown back again on his own speculation. Might it be, he wondered, that Owenie Garrigan had known someone by the name of Humphrey Deegan, a neighbour or fellow-parishioner at home in Ireland, maybe? And since one is more likely to be assaulted by an acquaintance than by a stranger could it be that at some time in the past young Garrigan had indeed been given a black eye by a man called Humphrey Deegan? But then what strange gift of telepathy enabled Owenie Garrigan to transmit this seemingly inconsequential message? Owenie Garrigan who was so tongue-tied as to be almost mute!

Alternatively, Schnitzer asked himself, was the subconscious mind capable of ideas and images independent of things perceived or apprehended? Was – *pace* Freud! – the intellect capable of pure creation unfettered by the limitations of perception and experience? The notion excited the poet, stimulating the great surge of creativity that put *Who is Humphrey Deegan?* on the bookstalls within a year and threw the world of Gaelic literature into such a ferment. It did all that and more, but it did not exorcise the ghost of Humphrey Deegan, nor alleviate the bleak hopelessness that cries so poignantly from the opening lines:

Across the arid pastures of a dream
in lunar landscapes where no solace bides
the tortuous shapes of beckoning phantoms fade
– sandcastles, melting in the uncaring tide –
to form again, refashioned with cruel art
that lures the faltering seeker, stumbling still,
a witless boy who'd drain the heaving sea
with one small
shell . . .

Schnitzer continued to be obsessed with the dream that never dimmed or faded but stayed as fresh in his mind as the night he dreamt it, and in time he came to wonder if it was not Humphrey Deegan (given that it was mathematically probable that there was someone, somewhere, by that name) who possessed the powers of telepathy which he had been attributing to Owenie Garrigan. And from here, of course, it wasn't such a long step to considering the possibility of contacting the shadowy Humphrey Deegan. A perusal of the Greater London Telephone Directory and of the electoral rolls revealed nothing but sometimes Schnitzer would be arrested by a face on a busy street or in the crowded Underground and be gripped by a wild, irrational hope that it was the face of the one he sought: the fixation continued to grow until in the end the poet would be seized by the compulsion to approach the total stranger (politely to be sure) and ask his name. The compulsion was a dangerous one as may be imagined: one day in Bond Street a bowler-hatted city gent, affronted by what he took to be a vagrant's presumption, raised his brolly as though to strike the poet; and a compatriot of Schnitzer's laying gas mains in Tottenham Court Road became foully abusive when asked the same question. The spectre of Humphrey Deegan would be exorcised in time: but in a way that O'Shea could not have foreseen and would hardly have welcomed if he had.

OPINIONS WERE sharply divided over *Who is Humphrey Deegan?* and the polarization of views that began with the publication of *Doulton Glaze* intensified with Schnitzer's third collection of verse. Vidor T. Whitmere spoke of the Dali-like quality of the imagery in the title poem and other critics saw in it a brave effort to confront the *alter ego*, citing in evidence that cryptic little fragment called "I" (*Who is Humphrey Deegan?* p 56):

Am I
the I
I
think
I
am?

"The poet has caught a deep metaphysical notion here with the minimum of words," wrote Fr Alban Ó Gallóglaigh in the *Maynooth Magazine*, "an economy which seems almost a presage of silence. There is a profound spirituality in O'Shea's latest work: what the early Irish monks sought in retreat and solitude O'Shea seeks in the teeming heart of the city – the quest is the same and the Glenbeg poet can be as alone in Trafalgar Square or in Piccadilly Circus as Robinson Crusoe on his desert island. For O'Shea there is no circus in Piccadilly. Which is not to say that his introspection is akin to the navel-gazing narcissism of the pampered youth of today seeking an easy short-cut to spiritual understanding; the one is the merest indulgence, the transient fascination of a plastic rattle for a drooling infant – the other is the authentic hunger for truth."

Not all critics were so favourable. In a remarkably sour review which he wrote for *Aquarius*, Dr Claude Prendeville of the Chair of Modern Gaelic Poetry in Trinity College, Dublin, dismissed *Who is Humphrey Deegan?* as "a farrago of sub-Berkeleyian nonsense" and wondered what Rónán Mac Rónáin and Banba Books were up to. If it was some kind of obscure joke it was a very damp squib indeed, Dr Prendeville went on, and licensed buffoons were no longer fashionable in the world of letters. *Milestones* had a certain naive appeal and there were some almost Betjeman-like evocations of the London scene in *Doulton Glaze*; but this latest offering, Dr Prendeville declared, was pure unadulterated bosh; pretentious bosh at that!

Critics of prose and poetry alike frequently confound their readers with conflicting views on the merits of an author's work: a novel which is highly acclaimed in the literary pages of the *Sunday Times* may be dismissed as garbage by the *Observer* and reviewers' judgements are so often false that one can only marvel that they retain any credibility at all. There was no dearth of correspondents to rush to the defence of Schnitzer while as many more rallied to support Dr Prendeville in the long and acrimonious exchange that filled the letters page of the *Irish Times* for several weeks (boosting the paper's circulation considerably in the process) and which was taken up with equal fervour in other papers and periodicals; and while none of this bothered O'Shea in the least he was very bothered indeed by the attention it focused on him in his London retreat.

The Rowton house had suited Schnitzer O'Shea admirably for it was the ideal place for one who wished to remain unnoticed, a community where the little foibles of others were accepted with a toleration that was truly civilized, where

154

understanding was extended with a fine generosity of spirit. Thus if Schnitzer felt impelled to cry "Omophagy!" or some such word as he strode along the corridors nobody took much notice any more than the poet himself would have presumed to remark on another's behaviour. But the anonymity which he so prized was rudely snatched from him when a team from Radio Telefís Éireann arrived one day to do a half-hour feature for the *Poets in Exile* series, with Schnitzer as the subject. If the programme had been in the hands of anyone but Aengus Mac Proinsias it is virtually certain that Schnitzer would have refused to take part but in the face of Aengus's smiling persuasion he agreed reluctantly and for the next couple of days the camera trailed him all over London with all the persistence of an Apache scout in the pay of the US cavalry. Schnitzer was filmed sitting with the winos and cider-addicts in Shepherd's Bush Green; he was shown deep in the study of *Group Psychology and the Analysis of the Ego* in the Lambeth public library; emerging from Arlington House in the morning to begin his day's wanderings and drinking a cup of tea from a market stall in Ladbroke Grove.

It was a rather trying time for the poet, a sore distraction from the meditative life he had embraced, but there was worse to follow for no sooner had the programme gone out on television than he became the unwilling recipient of shoals of letters, many of them invitations to talk on his life and work from such diverse groups as the Inisfallen Society, which met in the plush Tara Hotel in Kensington, and the Connolly Association, in its rather musty little premises in Gray's Inn Road – not to mention the Clann na hÉireann-sponsored CRAC*, Green Ink Writers Group, the Troops Out Movement, the Irish in Britain Representation Group and one or two of the more adventurous county associations. Not all of the letters were invitations, however; quite a few were from struggling poets and writers all over Britain asking for advice or assistance, and a minority were venomously-worded missives that denounced him as a disgrace to his country, one who had done more harm to the image of the Irish abroad than all the brawling navvies since the day of Moleskin Joe. One,

* Ceol, rinnce, amhránaíocht, cómhrá – *Music, dancing, singing, conversation; a sort of Peoples' Festival held annually in Birmingham.*

which was unstamped and signed merely "Respectable Irish Mother", threatened that if ever their paths crossed she would bash his face in with whatever implement was nearest to hand.

Schnitzer ignored the letters, invitations and threats alike, but it was becoming clear to him now that he would have to move, that Arlington House no longer afforded the protection he had so long enjoyed. For whatever shred of privacy the *Poet in Exile* series might have left him was dispelled by a prominent article, together with a very fine photograph of his head and shoulders, that appeared in the *Irish Post* around this time. The article, headed *Camden Town Laureate* was written by Hank Folan, the *Poet's* outspoken columnist who claimed that O'Shea belonged to the Irish in Britain more than he did to the Irish at home and urged the Irish community at large to honour him accordingly. It is true that some sections of the Irish community needed no such urging, but there were others who took a very different view of things and the prestigious Irish Club in Eaton Square was rocked to its very foundations in a row that blew up over the poet. One of the letters which Schnitzer received before he left the Rowton house was from the cultural committee of the club asking if he would give a poetry reading there as part of the St Patrick's Day festivities they were planning. The poet did not reply, of course, but at a subsequent meeting where the arrangements were being discussed the charismatic building contractor Mr P. J. (Padjoe) Kilallagan threatened to cancel his club membership if the invitation to O'Shea were not rescinded. In a forceful appeal the ageing building contractor, an impressive figure in spite of his years, argued that far from wanting to honour someone like O'Shea they should disown him completely. Genius he might well be, old Padjoe declared, but the man they had seen on the *Poets in Exile* series, shuffling about London in a tattered overcoat and consorting with the winos in Shepherd's Bush, such a man did nothing but damage to the image of the Irish abroad and it didn't matter a tuppenny damn if he was the greatest poet since Brian O Higgins! Waxing eloquently reminiscent, the contractor recalled when he himself first came over from Ireland back in the 1920s, at a time when there were a dozen strong men begging for every available job, and how – he wouldn't put a tooth in it! – not having the train

156

fare when he got off the Liverpool boat (a cattle-boat at that: no Aer Lingus flights for working men in those days!) he had tramped southwards working at whatever he could get along the way, a few days with a farmer here, a week's navvying there, a couple of shifts stoking in a gasworks somewhere else; until finally, footsore and weary, he arrived in the metropolis. Like Dick Whittington before him, old Padjoe told the meeting with a wry little smile, he had not found the streets of London to be paved with gold, but by dint of hard work and business acumen he had built up his own little empire, giving employment to hundreds of his compatriots in the process and (though he hesitated to remind them!) not being ungenerous with the club when occasion demanded. He too could have gone for the easy option, old Padjoe said, he could have chosen the soft life of the drifting layabout: except that he was too full of the pride of kith and kin and country to let himself down like that. Deprivation, for him, was the spur that had driven him to get on in the world, not an excuse to wallow in the gutter. And so it was that beginning with only the most rudimentary equipment – a pick-axe, a shovel or two, and an old wheelbarrow left carelessly behind by a borough council road gang – he had risen to become a household name in the construction industry. *That,* old Padjoe suggested, was the kind of accomplishment that the Irish abroad should aim for, rather than make spectacles of themselves for any television company, English or Irish. In conclusion, the contractor said that it would be an insult to their patron saint who would be so fittingly honoured by their Irish-American cousins on 17 March to have a dosser like O'Shea taking part in the festivities.

In the face of such determined opposition it is not altogether surprising that the invitation was formally withdrawn and a tactfully-worded letter was despatched to the poet to this effect.

Schnitzer did not receive this letter, however, for by now he had moved from Camden Town to squat in a damp basement in an area of Westbourne Park that was ripe for demolition.

❧❧ Chapter Fourteen. ❧❧

S CHNITZER O'SHEA WAS now enjoying what most respectable members of society never achieve: true liberation. For the poet was as free as anyone in a complex and interdependent civilization can hope to be. He was beholding to no one and no one had any claim on him; he paid no rent, he clocked no card and he went where he would, when he would. His wants were minimal and if, on a warm summer's night when the London sky was suffused with a yellow glow and the hum of traffic lulled the ear, he felt disinclined to return to the crumbling Victorian terrace where he skippered with other liberated souls, he would stretch out in some park and sleep as soundly as the most pampered business executive in the Hilton Hotel. No longer addicted to cigarettes nor even tempted to drink the odd glass of beer, Schnitzer could get by very well on a diet of bread and tea, a bowl of soup in some little market cafe, or even a head of lettuce thrown to him by some big-hearted Cockney street trader. O'Shea asked next to nothing of society and therein lay his claim to freedom.

What occasional company the poet wished for he could find among one of the few sections of the community that would not look askance at his shabby appearance; the winos and cider-addicts, *habitués* of the parks and derelict sites who gathered in the lonely fraternity of misery to seek forgetfulness or to dull their senses in a bottle of cheap wine or a flagon of cider. Schnitzer would stretch out on the little patch of grass by Euston Station or it might be on Shepherd's Bush Green, among the wine and cider drinkers, never accepting the proferred bottle himself, for he had no longer any use for alcohol, but relaxed and at ease among those who made no demands on him though the price of a bottle of Strongbow he would never begrudge them. Some critics have said that the poet's egotism precluded any feelings of sympathy for others less fortunate than himself but this is to misunderstand the character of O'Shea completely. For Schnitzer did not see the wine and cider drinkers as the flotsam and jetsam which

159

society has labelled them (far less would he entertain the word "dregs"!) nor would it occur to him, ever, to consider them as being any worse off than some middle-class suburbanite enslaved by a regular job, marriage and a mortgage. O'Shea, in truth, paid the park alcoholics the supreme compliment of *not* feeling sorry for them, a compliment they appreciated instinctively. The simple act of stretching out on the grass in their midst on a sunny day, or huddling with them in a dank cellar when it rained spoke more than a thousand homilies or exhortations to reform – more, even, than the unwelcome ministry of the well-disposed. A man was a man for a' that in Schnitzer's book.

The poet's liberation was not total, however, and perhaps no mortal ever achieves complete liberation; not the monk in his spartan cell, nor the Oriental mystic subjecting his body to the most extreme disciplines, starvation, flagellation or whatever. He was still plagued by that "pike-like hunger unassuaged", by the *unknowability* of so much, the incalculable vastness of knowledge that could never be encompassed, not even by the most sophisticated computer devised by man. There were whole vistas of knowledge of which he had not even caught a glimpse, Schnitzer knew, and beyond them stretched further vistas still. The unattainability of that which he craved lay like a monstrous burden on the poet and time and again it calls forth from the pages of his massive poem-novel like the cry of a lost soul. Eventually, and inevitably, the poet came to accept that the sum total of human knowledge must always stand in relation to the sum total of human ignorance, as a molehill stands in relation to Mount Everest; Schnitzer came, unavoidably, to the bleak realization that if he lived for a thousand years and devoted every waking moment to the holy quest for knowledge he would still, at the end of it all, be as far as ever from the shimmering goal of omniscience. Truth, he realized in the end, could only be apprehended in a fragmentary and indeed sometimes contradictory way, like gathered shards that defy all efforts to assemble them together again in their original pattern.

A Cry From the Pit was to be Schnitzer O'Shea's final statement, the presage of silence that Fr Ó Gallóglaigh in the *Maynooth Magazine* had himself so shrewdly presaged. Into this gargantuan work of more than a thousand pages he would cram everything of life that he could, as if rendering a last account: and thereafter he would withdraw into a state of purposeful non-cognition, shutting out all external influences from his mind as far as was humanly possible and seeking to live on a purely corporal level. The wish to do this is expressed with considerable power in the thirteenth canto of *A Cry From the Pit* (p 534):

> And so to drift unfeeling, comatose*
> as floats the limpid starfish billowing
> through some deep pool of lulling lambency,
> or teeming plankton, current-borne
> insentient in the vastness of the sea

It is perhaps the clearest expression of the poet's yearning for the luxury of mindless peace, the bliss of a purely physical existence. And in passing it is of interest to note that Vidor T. Whitmere in his lengthy appraisal of *A Cry From the Pit* believes that O'Shea, having reached the peak of his development as a poet, would go on to experiment with newer forms, divorcing words from meaning to use them for purely aural effect as a composer of a symphony arranges musical notes. The notion deserves some consideration though it is difficult to imagine Schnitzer wanting to compose when he had no longer anything to say; as against that it must be admitted that he pushed the meaning of words to the limit and beyond in the long dream sequence that contains the lines:

> The yellow dawning, gauzy as a veil
> of mellow somnolence in viscous flow
> that bathes the verdant vales of *Tír na nÓg***
> Ambrosia's largesse.

It would be difficult to see in these lines anything other than the formless imagery of a dream though, to be sure, students of the *Pit* have dismembered and scrutinized them for hidden meaning. Professor Heinrich Mannerbaum of the Chair of Celtic Studies in Stuttgart University laughed to scorn this propensity of the thesis-writers for discovering meanings which the poet never intended to convey. Only in a dream, Dr Mannerbaum argues, could the gauziness of a veil be related to

---

* *The Irish word* támhach, *in the original, is rather more expressive and the line* "Ar snámh sa tsruth to támhach faon" *is weakened in translation.*
** *The mythical Land of Youth.*

viscosity, and "Ambrosia's largesse" is quite meaningless!

A *Cry From the Pit* was written on a massive old-fashioned ledger bound in leather and with a brass clasp which Schnitzer rescued from a refuse bin outside a prestigious firm of tailors and cutters in London's West End; the work runs to over a thousand printed pages and is divided into fifty cantos of varying lengths. It was fortunate indeed that Schnitzer came on so compact and durable a supply of writing material for if the work had been written on loose sheets the probability is that it would not have survived in its entirety at all; in fact it may well be that it was the sight of the huge old ledger with its sturdy covers and marbled page-edging which moved the poet to begin his massive work.

Critics have wrangled somewhat pointlessly as to whether *A Cry From the Pit* is primarily a novel in poetic form or a poem in the shape of a novel (and Pacelli O'Mahoney, in *Trowel & Templet*, couldn't resist the easy jibe of calling the work a "povel!"): it is both in equal measure, rather as if Joyce's *Ulysses* had been written in verse. The quality of the poetry is almost unfalteringly good throughout, a sustained *tour-de-force* indeed, and the personae are observed with all the clinical detachment of a bacteriologist studying micro-organisms under a glass slide. "Murder your darlings," was the advice given by the Englishman Quiller Couch to aspiring writers, but O'Shea has no darlings among the characters of his epic work; nor villains, either. What the poet has done, of course, is to stand the popular concept of the novel on its head to give us something that is at once rather more and rather less than the conventional form of the genre. For as Vidor T. Whitmere makes clear in his *Poet in Hobnails*, "O'Shea contemptuously eschews both plot and progress in this great, unwieldy hunk of work; there is no beginning and no end – indeed one may question if there is a 'middle'!"

Whitmere is right for Schnitzer was quite uninterested in clever-clever plot construction, less still would he allow himself to be bound by fictional probabilities.* His technique, as Ruane Mac Éamainn pointed out in a lecture delivered to the Merriman Society, is that of omnivision, of the robotic camera

---

* *"Life is not committed to fictional probabilities,"* from The Climate of Love by Monk Gibbon.

with full rotation, missing nothing, indefatigable and terrifyingly honest. "O'Shea," said Mac Éamainn, "presents us with great – one might almost say *indigestible* – dollops of life, devoid (as so much of life is devoid) of any discernible pattern or purpose . . . But it is life vibrant and lusty, an untended garden where flowers and weeds alike flourish in riotous profusion: not the ordered selectivity of the cemetry lawn!"

Yes to be sure, but perhaps the most revolutionary concept of the *Pit* is to be found in the interchangeability of the characters, as for example when "A" becomes "B" or "C" becomes "A" in what at first seems to be the most arbitrary caprice. This is a startlingly fresh concept and there can be little doubt that Schnitzer employed the device to stress what he saw as the corporeal nature of humanity with the individual a mere component, as replaceable as any piece of throw-away equipment in our criminally wasteful society. Vidor T. Whitmere considers that the poet just may have been indulging in a little Joycean leg-pulling here, an interesting enough conjecture but one which is belied, surely, by the sombre tone of the work as a whole.

The two interchangeable characters we most often encounter in *A Cry From the Pit* are Brendan Thale and Tony Barr* and it is never quite clear whether we are dealing with two separate people or with two facets of the same character. We come upon Brendan Thale in the first canto standing at the entrance to Mornington Crescent tube station and ruminating on the human condition:

To serve that sentence, unreprieved
existence-bound from that first fateful step
when passion's** need wrought irreversibly
what even Death may not revoke unless
it be that Death is truly named and he
is final with such sweet finality
as brooks no doubting – Nirvana's nothingness!

The use of "sweet" to qualify "finality" sets the tone of the work and gives some inkling of the poet's longing for that

---

* A play on words: Brendan Thale (Bréan den tSaol) means "Sick of life" and Tony Barr (Tóin ná Bárr) means "Head nor tail". Perhaps Vidor T. Whitmere is right and Schnitzer was having a little sly fun!
** Macna in the original, a rather more earthy connotation.

"sweet oblivion" that crops up a few lines farther along, but it is difficult to reconcile the anti-life sentiments with the picture of Brendan Thale in his flash blue suit, winkle-picker shoes and the Panatella cigar he draws on with such relish as he considers the prospect of an evening's enjoyment; a drink in the Mother Black Cap up the way, the dance in the Buffalo Ballroom in Chalk Farm Road or a game of Twenty Five with some of his mates over in Finsbury Park. This is the stuff of life, not death, and the choice of time and setting (early evening, symbolizing a beginning, and the Underground station with its suggestion of movement and travel) would seem to have been chosen with deliberate care in order to counterpoint the grim note of mortality. Brendan Thale commits suicide in the twenty-seventh canto but we meet him again a mere twenty pages farther on when it is suggested that it was Tony Barr who had taken his own life by walking under the No 73 (Stoke Newington) bus in Euston Square. To complicate matters further Tony Barr turns up hale and hearty in canto forty-five, employed now as a street-orderly by the Lambeth Borough Council and planning to marry a winsome little Vietnamese girl he met at an anti-communist rally in Hyde Park. What difference, O'Shea seems to say, whether it was Brendan Thale or Tony Barr who died, their place in the scheme of things is so insignificant as not to matter.

The poet would seem to be making this point more obliquely in the shattering little cameo in the middle of the twenty-third canto where a group of children look briefly up from their game of hopscotch at a passing funeral . . . distracted, the children lose track of the score and a virulent squabble ensues as the hearse, followed by a black limousine with its two official mourners, rolls quietly past. Brendan Thale's death (or is it Tony Barr's?) is caused by despair, by the terrible sense of loss he feels in not being able to recall every moment of his life:

Oh, could some pen infallible
each instant of his life in full record
with due exactitude, each fleeting thought
and all that came within perception's ken!

One thinks inescapably here of Marcel Proust's À la Recherche du Temps Perdu, of the chimera of total recall, but above and beyond all else the note which recurs most often in

164

the *Pit* is the longing to escape into some imagined world or state of being that would combine the warm security of the pre-nativity with the quiet seclusion of the grave; as far back as *Milestones* Schnitzer spoke of the "womb-dark, tomb-dark hall", and he returns to the theme again and again in lines like the following:

And so to come through bleak Foreboding's fog
depression's melancholic load to shed;
at last to lie, of all encumbrance free
in some warm, night-black world, grave-quiet and still
of sweet unknowingness . . . .

Like all great works of art *A Cry From the Pit* may be appreciated on different levels. Taken at its most superficial it is a chronicle of surpassing interest, a meticulously-wrought mosaic of place and period, a vivid evocation of London scenes, vignettes of such arresting power and beauty that even in translation they bring a lump to the throats of Londoners the world over with lines like, "By Tower Bridge the Thames' quiescent flow" or "Oxford Street, turned festive in the sun". But then there are ascending layers of awareness, the feeling of being drawn upwards towards some revelation, of being dazzled and enchanted by the sheer voluptuousness of the work, the psychedelic bombardment of sensations and images until the mind reels from a surfeit of beauty. Above all, however, it is what Dr Heinrich Mannerbaum in his fine work* calls "the most fascinating safari that any artist can embark upon – the exploration of the inner self."

A CRY FROM *the Pit* was penned in conditions that would have deterred any but the most dedicated artist. For the poet was sleeping rough all through the writing of his masterpiece, moving from one dilapidated Victorian terrace to another before the remorseless advance of the bull-dozer and the demolition gangs. O'Shea had none of the facilities associated in the popular mind with the business of literary creation, no table (let alone desk!) on which to rest his weighty ledger, nor any form of heating other than that which he could

* O'Shea and the Pit: A Key. *Published by Heinemann in London and New York.*

procure by burning odd bits of firewood or wainscotting ripped from the mouldering walls. When Schnitzer wrote by night it can only have been in the flickering light of a candle stuck in an old beer bottle with the smell of decay and ruin all round him and the occasional intrusion of some other vagrant plaguing him with questions about his work. And then of course there was the inconvenience of having to lug the heavy ledger about with him wherever he went, an incommodious burden but one which he dare not leave from him for any length of time for fear that it would not be there when he returned. Wherever he went Schnitzer carried the ledger in a plastic shopping bag and soon he became a familiar sight round the area as he sat on a park bench scribbling furiously or toted his epic work about with him on his long walks.

This was not without its hazards for apart altogether from the risk of having the work stolen there was a danger of attracting unwelcome attention now that the IRA had begun to extend its activities to the British capital. Not surprisingly a certain paranoia began to manifest itself among ordinary citizens who had no particular wish to depart this life prematurely and who, consequently, began to regard plastic shopping bags and holdalls with a degree of suspicion. In point of fact the poet came close to losing his *magnum opus* one evening as he made his way back to his skipper in Westbourne Park. This happened in Ladbroke Grove where three youths suddenly blocked his path and demanded to know what he was carrying; in a roughly jocular manner, to be sure, but with an unmistakable suggestion of menace nonetheless. The youths were of the cultural sub-grouping commonly refered to as "bovvers", underprivileged members of the working class whose experience of life may not have been conducive to the nicest behaviour; and in the manner of youngsters everywhere they were out for a bit of fun.

The trio – a skinny little chap with a shorn skull and three waxed hair spikes, an overweight fellow festooned with swastikas and other Nazi insignia, and a hefty six-footer whose massive arms were adorned with a multiplicity of tattoos – challenged the poet as to the contents of his bag and the poet ventured to suggest that it was none of their business. The bovvers, however, thought otherwise.

"Come on, Pat, wot you got in the bag? Give us a shufti."

166

"There's a good chap, Patrick, open the bag!"

"Like now, sunshine!"

"No dice, chaps," Schnitzer said, borrowing an expression from his picture-going days. "The bag stays shut."

"The hell it does," said the six-footer in a John Wayne drawl, at the same time making what might be construed as a threatening gesture.

"The bag stays shut," Schnitzer repeated and sought to pass on. But the trio were a solid block before him now and he got nowhere.

"Open it, Pat! Don't act the ape, " the fat one said with an air of strained patience.

"Open it or we do!" the skinny one with the waxed spikes said less patiently.

It may well have been that if Schnitzer had obliged them the bovvers would have let him off with a bit of friendly abuse but he did not care to take the risk, seemingly. At all events he again refused.

"I'm not opening the bag, chaps," he told them with quiet finality and tightened his grip on the plastic carrier.

"Not much, you ain't!" the skinny one said, reaching for the bag.

"We can't have that, Patrick," said the overweight fellow, "No way!"

"Not for one f——— moment," chimed in the biggest of them, using an unprintable adjective.

"Piss off," said the poet, adopting their vernacular.

It was a stalemate but the bovvers considered one last appeal before, as the big fellow threatened, they got physical. "You see, Patrick, it ain't just idle curiosity on our part – is it, chums?"

"No way!" chorused the other two.

"It's more like a duty. It's our bounden duty to inspect suspicious parcels, Pat, bundles like you got there in the bag."

"Suspicion, like beauty, reposes in the eye of the beholder," the poet said, but the boys were not impressed.

"You see, Patrick, we ain't accusing *you* of nuffink . . . "

"No way!"

"It ain't that we suspect *you* of being a bomber, but what with all those other loony Paddies running about with suspicious parcels, planting bombs in caffs and old peoples' homes

167

and things, well, stone the crows, Pat, we can't have that sort of thing, can we?"

"Bleedin' true, we can't!"

"You read the police notices about being alert and all that: you *can* read, can't you, Patrick?"

Schnitzer declined to reply and the skinny punk took over.

"Just imagine, Pat . . . some poor old dear pops out to her local for a glass of mild and a bit of a chin-wag with some other old granny . . . and then you come along with your bomb, and 'woof!' the boozer's blown sky-high and the poor old dear along with it!"

"Have you thought about *that*, Patrick?" asked the over-weight one sadly.

"Thought is the proof of existence. I think therefore I am," Schnitzer replied, quoting Descartes.

It is unlikely that a philosophical discussion would have followed this statement but in any case there was an interruption just then – an inebriated Hibernian staggered out of the Elgin Arms across the road and began haranguing the three bovver boys, telling them to let the poet go on his way. The intrusion was resented as one may imagine and after a very brief consultation with his two colleagues the fat boy went across to the drunken Irishman and head-butted him in the face, warning him at the same time that more serious injury would result if he didn't learn to keep his filthy hooter out of other folks' affairs. The Irishman subsided on the pavement, moaning in self-pity, and the overweight bovver rejoined the others, in no mood now for any further opposition.

"The bag, Patrick," he said, extending his hand imperiously.

"Yes, Patrick, the bag!" said the others.

The poet's reply to this was an agile and very well-placed kick that made the biggest of the three bovvers double over in agony, clutching his credentials; and then, with an over-arm movement which the fastest of bowlers might envy, he brought the massive ledger down with a resounding whack on the head of the skinny bovver, flattening his laquered spikes in the process. But by this time the overweight bovver had grabbed the poet in a crushing embrace, smashing his broad expanse of forehead into his victim's face at the same time. O'Shea was inured to hardship from an early age and it may well be that his threshold of pain was higher than average but at all events, he

168

took the head-butting better than his compatriot across the way and succeeded in extricating himself from the bear-like grip of the punk. This the poet managed to do by the perhaps not altogether sporting expedient of biting his opponent's adam's-apple. The fat bovver emitted a panicky scream and released his grip on Schnitzer in order to determine what degree of injury had been done to his thyroid cartilage, and the poet, thinking that he had better leave nothing to chance, brought his own cranial tactics to bear, butting his enemy in the solar-plexus with all the force of a sledge-hammer. The bovver collapsed like a half-set blancmange and with an exultant yell of *Vae victis!** Schnitzer walked off, still in possession of his precious manuscript.

* *Woe to the vanquished. It is not to be supposed that Schnitzer knew much more Latin than such familiar tags.*

❦❦❦ *Chapter Fifteen.* ❦❦❦

A CRY FROM *the Pit*, as befitted a work of its magnitude, was launched with much ceremony in Dublin, the publishers sparing no expense in the provision of food and drink for the literary folk who thronged the reception room of the Bailey, clamourous as a flock of gulls. The poet himself was not present.

Indeed, even if Schnitzer had wanted to attend the launching of his poem-novel he would not have been at liberty to do so, for by then he was in the custody of the police awaiting trial on a very serious, if quite preposterous charge. In the interval between the completion of *A Cry From the Pit* and his arrest, a period of eighteen months or so, Schnitzer withdrew more and more into himself, forsaking his meandering walks and his hours of study in the public libraries, to spend all his time riding round and round on the Underground, covering hundreds of miles every day yet never getting any farther than Morden or Cockfosters. For the poet had now abandoned his search for the Holy Grail of comprehensible truth and had begun to aspire instead to an amoebic level of existence, to cultivate that blissful state of non-cognition, the condition of tranquility which only death can surpass. Schnitzer had long achieved a degree of freedom not enjoyed by many and the petty problems of everyday living, the irritations and frustrations that are part and parcel of what is so oddly termed the rat race, impinged on him not at all. O'Shea had reduced the demands of existence to a minimum, like an Indian fakir, without quite relinquishing his hold on life, shutting out all that went on around him and retreating into the "mellow somnolence" he so craved. Schnitzer's goal was now the "ecstasy of the infinitude of space"; which ecstasy, his reading of the Tibetan mystics had told him, could be gained only by the most resolute dismissal of every form of distraction, and preferably in total darkness.

A homeless man, occupying the cellar of a demolished house, the poet could hardly afford the luxury of a private room, but in the London Underground he discovered a passable substitute. A state of near-hypnosis could be induced, Schnitzer discovered, by the repetitive pattern of sound and movement, the low whine that mounted to a barrage of noise, the metronomic swaying of the train, the glare of light and colour that alternated with the stygian darkness of the tunnel. All this was admirably conducive to a state of diminished awareness and it is likely that given time the poet would have mastered the techniques of suspended animation, the ability to enter a comatose condition that would come as close to non-being as is possible for the living. What more suitable place for the experiment than the London Underground where, except for the shabbiness of his appearance, the poet would not have looked very different from any of the other passengers who sat, motionless as so many corpses, staring blankly before them as the tube rumbled from stop to stop? The picture is conveyed very well by Schnitzer in "Northern Line" (*Doulton Glaze* p 71):

> The whispered sigh
> soft
> as a turning leaf
> in Blunden's Wood*
> teasing the ear – a pledge that's quick-redeemed!
> A silver worm from out the tunnel's eye
> ejects its silent swarm, inanimate
> through
> automated
> doors – a
> multifarious birth (Homoncular!)
> of full-grown human beings, and then
> the fading whine, ghost-wailing through the
> tunnel's winding way
> (the stark Plutonic dark)
> Morden, Euston, Golder's Green . . .
> I drink Idris** when I'se dry!

It is not to be thought, however, that the poet encountered no problems at all in this quest for dissociation, in his attempt

---

* *A wood in Co Kilkenny. The American Walbark sees in such odd references to home evidence of what he calls the "exile syndrome". Tosh!*

**The reference is to an advertisement, once common on the Underground.*

172

to withdraw into himself to the exclusion of all else, for like the saint who falls from grace now and then, or the reformed drunkard who yields occasionally to his old weakness, or indeed (at the risk of indelicacy!) the aged male whose libido may revive alarmingly from time to time, O'Shea would sometimes be filled with a sudden and irresistible urge to feel and think again, to utter some exotic word or to pursue once more the spectral Humphrey Deegan. Thus he might cry *Quadrinominal!* or *Ascititious!* as he came out of his self-induced trance, and none of his fellow-passengers would take more than a passing notice; indeed almost any behaviour, however odd, might be tolerated on the Underground so long as it made no direct demands on those travelling there. A blind eye could be turned on a West Indian lady arguing furiously with herself, or on a truculent young skinhead flexing his tattooed muscles; a drunk might loll in his seat like a rubber dummy and an epileptic thrash about wildly on the floor; none of this would cause much consternation but it was a different matter when some passenger was confronted with a bearded tramp asking, however politely, if his name was Humphrey Deegan. That went beyond the limits of transgression, as great an embarrassment as the gaucherie of being offered a seat by a total stranger on the tube; a violation, in short, that made people feel threatened and insecure. And it was resented accordingly.

But impulses of this kind are not easily curbed and it was Schnitzer's misfortune that one day as he emerged from his torpor on the Circle Line he saw sitting across the corridor from him a man whose facial composition was unmistakably Irish. There was nothing unusual in this, to be sure, for London has always had a very sizeable Irish population, but unluckily for himself the poet was seized with an overpowering conviction that the man sitting opposite him was none other than the elusive Humphrey Deegan. It was a conviction too strong to ignore or suppress and, rousing himself, Schnitzer went across to the man and asked him point blank if he *was* Humphrey Deegan.

As on previous occasions the response was none too cordial, but in this instance there was a discernible element of panic too, as well there might. For as anyone who followed the reports of Schnitzer's trial will remember, the man whom he confronted on the Underground that day was none other than the notorious "Demolisher" Duggan from Belfast, a member of an IRA active service unit who had gained his expertise in the use of explosives while serving with the Royal Engineers. And Duggan had reason enough to feel apprehensive just then for he was being tailed by two detectives from the Bomb Squad, one of whom was stationed strategically by each of the nearest two doors, ready to pounce on the bomber as soon as he made to leave the train. There was a debate under way even then in the house of Commons where the honourable members were discussing the sorry state of Duggan's native province, or to be more exact, that portion of his native province which came under their jurisdiction. Neither of the two detectives was naive enough to imagine that Volunteer Duggan was on his way to Westminster to listen to the debate and pleased as they were at the imminence of his capture they must have thought that Fortune was being lavishly generous when they saw the poet take a seat beside their man and begin conversing with him animatedly. It was as plain as the nose on your face, as the detectives saw it, that Duggan had an accomplice and this was their rendezvous! And this suspicion was confirmed to their satisfaction very shortly.

Up to this moment the Demolisher had been fully occupied with thoughts of escape, for of course it was clear to him that his visit to Westminster would have to be abandoned; he had, not unnaturally, been dismayed to find that the Bomb Squad was on to him but he must have felt that half of London was aware of his identity when he found himself being asked by a complete stranger if his name was Humphrey Deegan. There was after all, enough similarity between the two surnames to make the bomber think that others had recognized him, too.

"What makes you ask, son?" Volunteer Duggan asked in a very unfatherly manner.

"A hunch," Schnitzer confessed, "a mere hunch!"

"A hunch?" the bomber said doubtfully and the poet nodded.

"Are you Humphrey Deegan?"

"Humphrey?" queried the bomber who in his alarm had missed the first part of the name a moment before.

"Humphrey Deegan," Schnitzer bustled with impatience. "Are you he?"

Volunteer Duggan fiddled with the brown parcel he was carrying, playing for time. "Where did you get the Humphrey bit, son?" he asked in a somewhat kindlier tone of voice, his mind grappling with the situation. They were in St James' Park now and the next stop was Westminster. He did not relish the idea of riding round all day on the Circle Line, the more so as the brown paper parcel was timed to explode within the hour.

"A dream," the poet answered, to the other's furious confusion. "I dreamt that Owenie Garrigan told me that Humphrey Deegan gave him a black eye."

"A dream . . . Owenie Garrigan," Duggan said, covertly watching the two detectives. "A dream?"

"A most vivid dream," Schnitzer replied. "Poor Owenie there in the trench and his eye all black and swollen, and he told me that Humphrey Deegan had done it."

"He did?" Duggan hazarded, his mind racing.

The watching detective could not possibly have divined the sudden flash of inspiration that brightened the Demolisher's glum countenance.

"Well, bang on, old son! Oh, but you're the bright one and no mistake, sharp as a needle, kid! Yes, yes that's the monicker, friend, and I clocked the wee gulpin, smack in the peeper; deserved it too, the wee scut! Gave him a real shiner, Mack!"

The effect of all this on O'Shea may be readily imagined for it had ramifications he may not have been entirely willing to face up to: must this confirmation recall him from that cosy half-world where he spent so much time now, drifting comatose? The poet's predicament was not altogether unlike that of a scientist who stumbles on a discovery which, though fascinating and far-reaching in itself, is less than totally welcome because it disproves his own most cherished theories. Indeed one might even liken the poet to an invalid who gets a last-moment reprieve when he had become fully reconciled to passing on: Humphrey Deegan's existence must surely constitute a summons back to life and cerebreal activity again from the contentment of the nirvana-state he had been cultivating.

Schnitzer was still in a bemused condition when the train slid to a halt in Westminster; and at that same moment the Demolisher Duggan leapt to his feet, thrust his brown paper parcel into the poet's hands and with a loud, theatrical "Good-luck!" dived past the waiting detective and out the door. The detective gave instant chase, of course, while his colleague grappled with Schnitzer, but Duggan was gone, disappearing into the other train a split second before it pulled out. In vain the dismayed Bomb Squad man ran along the platform hammering frantically on the windows of the moving train. His quarry was safely away, though did he but know it his reprieve was to be a brief one. A week later Volunteer Duggan came to a sticky end when the bomb he was carrying in a plastic lunch box went off prematurely, thus fulfilling the Biblical prophecy that those who live by the sword shall perish by it too.

THE ARREST of Schnitzer O'Shea caused a sensation in literary circles and his trial was followed with avid interest by his compatriots at home and abroad. Astonishingly, there were many who took the charges at face value, marvelling at the cunning of the poet in assuming so effective a disguise for his nefarious purpose: those who regarded the purpose as nefarious, that is! An anonymous contributor to *An Phoblacht*** wrote a long ballad in the traditional mode extolling the selfless courage of O'Shea in engaging one of the squad men so that his confederate might escape; sensible people, of course, were aghast and appalled that the authorities could be guilty of such a monumental blunder. There were the usual charges of police brutality and much was made, in some quarters, of the fact that at the initial three-minute hearing Schnitzer displayed a number of facial injuries, contusions, a black eye and a missing tooth. It is notoriously difficult to get at the truth in these matters when allegations of ill-treatment are slung so recklessly about and when the authorities insist that the injuries in question are either self-inflicted or the result of the accused having strenuously resisted arrest and certainly O'Shea is not on record as having complained about rough treatment while awaiting trial.

As a matter of fact the poet was pensive rather than apprehensive following his arrest, and beyond insisting that the

---

* The Republic, *a bilingual Republican paper.*

man who had passed him the lethal parcel in the Underground was named Deegan and not Duggan he failed to show much concern at his situation at all.

"Duggan's the name, son," Detective Inspector Brown said wearily on the second day of the poet's interrogation. "D-u-g-g-a-n. But not to worry! A rose by any other name, eh? We know all about him, but who are the others?" Schnitzer was unable to be of any assistance here and of course the detectives took a dim view of his lack of co-operation.

"Don't make it worse for yourself, lad," the second detective – Detective Sergeant Alphonsus (Ali) O'Donoghue, himself of Irish extraction and a devout Roman Catholic – appealed to Schnitzer. "They've dropped you in it, son: they've scarpered!"

"All we want are *names*," Detective Inspector Brown said, absently tweaking the poet's ear. "It will help you in court."

Schnitzer remained silent. Detective Sergeant O'Donoghue appealed to him to do the decent thing. "You'll be saving lives, son," he entreated, and Detective Inspector Brown arched a caustic eyebrow to suggest that the saving of lives ranked very low on the poet's list of priorities.

"We can make it hard for you," Harry Brown sighed. "So very hard."

"Or easy," Ali O'Donoghue offered. "It's up to you, son."

"Your choice," Harry Brown said, kneading the lobe of Schnitzer's ear between thumb and forefinger.

Two days later little or no progress had been made, O'Shea adamantly refusing (as the detectives saw it) to divulge any names although he did, inadvertently, set them off on a wild-goose chase. This resulted when Detective Sergeant O'Donoghue sought to draw him out about Volunteer Duggan and Schnitzer insisted once again that the man's name was Deegan; and then, a little concerned perhaps by the distraught look on the detective's face, the poet added that he scarcely knew Deegan at all, that he had learned of his existence only through a dream.

"A dream?" Ali O'Donoghue said with a pained look, and Schnitzer related his dream.

The identity of Owenie Garrigan was quickly checked out, of course, and that unfortunate young man spent three very unhappy days helping the CID with their inquiries up in Northmanton before they were satisfied that he had no connection with the IRA or any other such group. The experience proved rather too much for the timid-natured Garrigan who, immediately he was released, packed his suitcase and returned to Ireland where he lives in a state of utter funk to this day, unable to see a policeman of any grade or standing without starting to tremble like an autumn leaf. His speech impediment, too, has worsened greatly: the hapless victims of the bombs are not the only casualties in cases like this!

In the course of his own interrogation Schnitzer was shown irrefutable photographic and documentary proof that the man who had handed him the brown paper parcel in the tube was indeed Oscar J. Duggan, known otherwise as "Demolisher" Duggan. The poet accepted this proof with mixed feelings but on being asked if he would not now consider revealing all he knew about the bomber and his other accomplices Schnitzer replied that since the man in question would appear to be Oscar J. Duggan all right he had to accept that Humphrey Deegan was the product of his own mind and in consequence he must bow to Sigmund Freud's contention that all dreams had a secret meaning, though he baulked at Freud's assertion that the dreams of adults could be traced, by way of analysis, to erotic wishes.

This proved altogether too much for Detective Inspector Harry Brown who uttered a broken sob and flung himself on the poet, pinning him to the floor and threatening to "swing for the bastard!"; a touch melodramatically since in common with all civilized countries Britain abolished capital punishment many years ago. It was only with the most tactful persuasion that Ali O'Donoghue managed to get his superior off the struggling poet, but to be fair O'Shea was none the worse for this little lapse on the part of the officer, nor did he bear a grudge over it.

The police were doomed to disappointment as regards to getting any information from Schnitzer, it never having occurred to them, seemingly, that he might not be in possession of the information they wanted; there was indeed a further disappointment when a search of the cellar he had been sleeping in revealed the ledger on which he had written A Cry From the Pit. The find was borne off triumphantly for both forensic and linguistic examination and for a day or two it

178

was hoped that the massive tome would turn out to be an invaluable asset in the fight against terrorism. A vain hope, of course, and again Detective Inspector Brown might have vented his chagrin on the author of the great work but that his colleague managed to dissuade him. Speaking strictly off the record later on, Detective Sergeant O'Donoghue expressed his belief that O'Shea had been given anti-interrogation training, possibly by IRA personnel who had spent a term in the British army in order to become acquainted with such techniques. How else, he asked, could the poet withstand the pressure that had been brought upon him to confess? Less complimentary, perhaps, Detective Inspector Brown declared that talking to the poet was like trying to hold a conversation with a hairy ainew, a reference, no doubt, to both his un-communicativeness and the hirsute condition of his face!

There were massive security precautions at the trial of Schnitzer O'Shea. Armed police were positioned strategically round the Old Bailey, while members of the SAS mingled unobtrusively with the crowd. A plea of "not guilty" was entered on the poet's behalf since he himself declined to plead one way or the other, but the defence made a rather poor fist of contesting the Crown's case. Mr Hetherington-Mathers, QC, for the Crown, contended that the accused was an extremely dangerous and pathological man. He had played a key role in the terrorist's bombing campaign, his cunning disguise allowing him to operate with impunity under the very eyes of the law. Just how many bombing missions O'Shea had played a vital part in was anyone's guess, the prosecution said, and he would still be free to continue his diabolical work but for the competence of the Bomb Squad in trailing him to his meeting-place with Duggan. O'Shea was an unrepentant and committed terrorist, Mr Hetherington-Mathers, QC, continued and because of his stubborn – indeed mule-like – refusal to assist the police in their enquiries the perpetrators of these outrages were still at large. And his guilt was compounded further by the fact that he was no gullible youth misled by the armchair generals: O'Shea was in fact a man of letters, a poet of some merit (albeit in the Erse language) who must have realized fully what he was about when he embraced the despicable business of terrorism. It would be an affront to all those who had suffered as a result of the activities of O'Shea and his wicked associates not to employ the full rigours of the law.

The law, robed in the august personage of Judge Wilmington-Chivvers, concurred. In the course of a lengthy summing-up the learned judge described the poet as a man of almost unbelieveable depravity, a man quite beyond redemption, a truly evil man who had shown not the slightest trace of remorse for his wicked deeds. He agreed with the prosecution, Judge Wilmington-Chivvers said that being a poet – in whatever language, and he had to confess that he thought the Erse language was long since extinct! – only made O'Shea's crimes all the more heinous, for people did not expect that kind of thing from poets. Poetry was about sunshine and beauty and lovely things, the judge declared, and quoting the first verse of "Daffodils" he asked if anyone could imagine William Wordsworth carting explosive substances about the Underground with him; or indeed that other great English poet who wrote "Where the bee sucks there suck I" – the immortal Bard of Avon? Methinks not, Judge Wilmington-Chivvers quipped in one of his rare attempts at levity, and if indeed the accused were a poet of some standing then his actions were more inexcusable still!

Throughout the entire trial Schnitzer remained quite impassive, totally unconcerned; and as with his previous court appearance in Northmanton this air of detachment did him no good at all.* His serene acceptance contributed no doubt to the severity of the sentence which Judge Wilmington-Chivvers passed on him: fifteen years imprisonment! But even this cruel punishment the poet received with apparent indifference, not so much as throwing a glance of acknowledgment to his anguished well-wishers in the public gallery, nor to Cathal Pádraig Ó Grianáin who created a disturbance and was summarily fined for calling the judge a cultural bigot and a disciple of the detestable Henry the Eighth who had instigated the policy of extinguishing the Gaelic tongue

The press – the popular newspapers in particular – had a field day of course, vying with one another in the sensation-

---

*But in his heart the poet understood the futility of trying to encompass in tattling words the history which brought him to Humphrey Deegan, of trying to explain; and in truth he did not care.

180

alism of their headlines. Gotcha! Bomber-Poet Gets Fifteen Years! screamed the *Sun*, while the *Daily Express's* headline read Life for the Bearded Bomber. The *Daily Mail* called Schnitzer, "The evil genius behind the London bombs" and a cartoon in the *London Evening Standard* showed a bearded tramp chewing a stub of pencil as he stared at a blank sheet of paper while a simian-featured terrorist fumed impatiently in the background; the caption to this read "Oi'l be wid ye now in a tick, Shamus – just give us a minnit to compose me 'Ode to a Buttercup' and I'll help ye assemble dat bomb, begorrah!"

The responsible papers treated the matter more soberly to be sure, *The Guardian* wondering if perhaps a miscarriage of justice had not occurred and *The Times* blaming the Irish educational system which harped on the wrongs, real or imagined, that the Emerald Isle had suffered at the hands of the Sceptred Isle over the centuries, thus motivating misguided people like the oddly named Schnitzer O'Shea to embark upon a futile and wicked course of action. The *Daily Telegraph* carried a long article on the ambivalence of many Irish men of letters towards violence, citing W. B. Yeats's poem "A Terrible Beauty" as an example. A predisposition towards violence was a basic flaw in the Irish character, the article stated, and it seemed to be Britain's misfortune to have to suffer the consequence of that flaw. But what was the answer? Short of towing their turbulent neighbour several hundred miles out in the Atlantic it was difficult to think of a solution.

Not surprisingly the left-wing press took a rather different view of things. The *Socialist Worker* carried a quite scurrilous attack on the character and probity of Judge Wilmington-Chivvers, making some very nasty innuendoes indeed as to his Lordship's sexual preferences, while in more measured tones the Communist *Morning Star* demanded a retrial. In the *Irish Post*, Hank Folan devoted his entire column to Schnitzer's trial, asserting in what was perhaps the finest piece of journalistic rhetoric to come from his pen that O'Shea had been sacrificed on the altar of political expediency like many an Irishman before him; and even Pacelli Ignatius O'Mahoney, writing his leader for *Trowel & Templet*, regretted that the poet's political illiteracy had led him to get involved in the urban guerilla scene. A Marxist analysis of the situation would have enabled the erstwhile hod carrier to see the pointlessness

181

of mere incendiarism and that change would only come about through mass political action. The task, O'Mahoney said, was to organize.

There was comment aplenty in the Irish press, of course, and an editorial in the *Kilkenny People* (to which Schnitzer had contributed some of his earliest verse) marvelled at the obtuseness of the British judiciary in convicting one so obviously innocent as the Muldowneyscourt poet: what hope could there be of any political initiative ever succeeding, the *People* asked, in the face of such colossal stupidity?

Muldowneyscourt had plenty to talk about too, with opinion being far from unanimous concerning the poet's innocence. At the cattle-mart in Kilkenny one day Lar Buggy and Fintan Bolger bumped into each other and when their business was concluded they repaired to Andy's Tavern in Rose Inn Street where, almost before he had blown the froth off his pint, Lar Buggy brought up the matter of Schnitzer's conviction as a bomber.

"I told you it wasn't safe having the likes of him about the place, didn't I, Bolger?"

"You did," Fintan Bolger replied, defensively.

"I told you it wasn't known what the likes of him would do if he took it into his head – didn't I?"

"You did," repeated Fintan Bolger grudgingly.

"I said ye were at risk wid the likes of him under the roof, didn't I now?"

"If you did itself that don't mane you were right," Fintan Bolger shot back loyally defending his old employee.

"So what do it mane?" demanded Lar Buggy in some irritation. "Wasn't the hoor caught red-handed plantin' bums beyant in London?"

"Not exactly," Fintan Bolger said, "Wasn't it how the other fella handed him the package in the train?"

"And to be sure he did!" Lar Buggy sniffed. "Ain't that the way they go on, meeting in secret and passing each other parcels! Oh you may as well admit it, Finny, I was right about that galoot from the start – talkin' to himself below in the field!"

"Oh faith then, he wasn't the first man that ever talked to himself in a field," Fintan Bolger objected, but Lar Buggy was adamant.

182

"Not shouting at the top of their voice like your man was! And the way he went on on the *Late Lately Show*, streelin' out nonsense to bate the band! Sure you're not going to tell me that man was right in the head?"

"There's a gradle* of difference between plantin' bums and talkin' to youself," Fintan Bolger loyally insisted, "And I don't believe O'Shea had hand, act or part in it! The man wouldn't hurt a fly: hadn't I him in the house all those years and never a wrong word out of him?"

"Begor then you were lucky! But wouldn't it be a nice how-do-you-do if he got up one night and murdered ye all in yeer beds? You'd have a different opinion of him then, so you would!"

"Well that'd be a different thing altogether," Fintan Bolger agreed reasonably and then went on to talk of other matters.

There was even more talk in Northmanton as may be imagined. Gladys Webb lost no opportunity to remind Mother Perkins that she kept some very odd company indeed and Mother Perkins – who was even more convinced than Fintan Bolger of Schnitzer's innocence – answered sharply that it was all stuff and nonsense and that she wouldn't believe a word of it, not in a month of Sundays.

"I daresay," Mrs Webb came back drily, "there's none so blind as them as won't see!"

"Only them as can't!" Lavinia retorted sharply. "Cor blimey, be your age Glad, it wouldn't be the first time the rozzers fitted someone up! Where you bin all your life, gal?"

"Well I ain't bin consorting with criminals and that's for sure!" Gladys Webb replied smugly. The argument grew steadily more nasty from there on with the predictable result that Mother Perkins was once again asked to leave the Hope & Glory and not to return.

B UT WHAT of the poet himself, so unjustly deprived of his liberty and with the prospect of fifteen years imprisonment before him, less whatever remission he might gain for good behaviour? Life is full of compensations, as somebody once remarked, and it must be said that Schnitzer did not regard the

* *Great deal, a colloquiasm peculiar to the area.*

loss of his physical freedom as a very great misfortune. Indeed it is questionable if his incarceration amounted to a punishment at all for in essence it was a life that differed little from that which he had been so contentedly leading in the London Underground, except for the element of choice which no longer bothered him and the loss of mobility which bothered him even less. On the credit side the poet had all his worldly needs supplied gratis: three adequate meals a day, a bed of his own (a luxury he had not enjoyed in Mother Perkins' house in Northmanton!) and, due to the over-crowded state of the prison, the freedom to lie on his bunk for twenty-three hours a day undisturbed. It was a life that suited Schnitzer admirably, a life even more conducive to his goal of withdrawal and passivity than any amount of riding round on the Circle Line, a life that was as near as he could possibly get to that state which he so yearned for in these few final lines from A Cry From the Pit:

> The badger snug-wrapped in his warm lair,
> the hedgehog in his quilt of withered leaves
> the fieldmouse sleeping through the silent days,
> the woodlouse curled in the rotting beam –
> these know the peace that wretched humans crave
> and find, at last, in tenanting the grave . . . .
> Ah, yes!

NEW FICTION FROM
BRANDON

The House by Leland Bardwell

"A book that is a positive gem; it shines with a lustre that glints not only in the mind, but in the heart and soul as well."
– *Sunday Press*

Night Shift by Dermot Bolger

"No Irish novelist since McGahern has been so obsessed with the poetics of love, death and sex. No Irish novelist has so brilliantly captured the suburban underbelly of the city, the crazy unofficial lives." – *Magill*

Baulox by Tony Cafferky

"For all its humour and funny incident, *Baulox* can be read as a serious warning to us all to hang on to our humanity and sense of anarchy despite what They say." – *In Dublin*

The Life of Riley by Anthony Cronin

"I have laughed more at *The Life of Riley* than at any other book I have ever read." – *The Irish Times*
Published in England, Scotland and Wales by Alison & Busby (hb) and Faber & Faber (pb).

Twist and Shout by Philip Davison

"Very alive and very funny." – *In Dublin*

Grounds by Pauline Hall

"An utterly unpretentious Bildungsroman of an Irish girl growing into womanhood in the fifties and sixties." – *The Irish Times*
"Some of the most stirring prose written by an Irish author in ages." – *Evening Press*

Banished Misfortune by Dermot Healy

"You know by the end of the book you have been reading a writer who matters . . . the mastery of the form breathes through every line." – *Daily Telegraph*
Published in England, Scotland and Wales by Alison & Busby.

Night in Tunisia by Neil Jordan

"*Night in Tunisia* is one of the most remarkable stories that I have read in Irish story-telling since, or indeed before, Joyce." – Sean O'Faolain

Owl Sandwiches by John B. Keane

Owl Sandwiches is John B. Keane in light-hearted form; it is John B. Keane the observer of foibles and the teller of tales of compellingly dubious veracity; it is John B. Keane the publican, leaning over the bar with a wink and a nod, and asking, "Did I ever tell you about the time . . . ?"

Boy With an Injured Eye by Ronan Sheehan

"Left me speechless with admiration." – *Evening Herald*
"A distinguished contribution to the renaissance of the Irish short story." – *Irish Press*

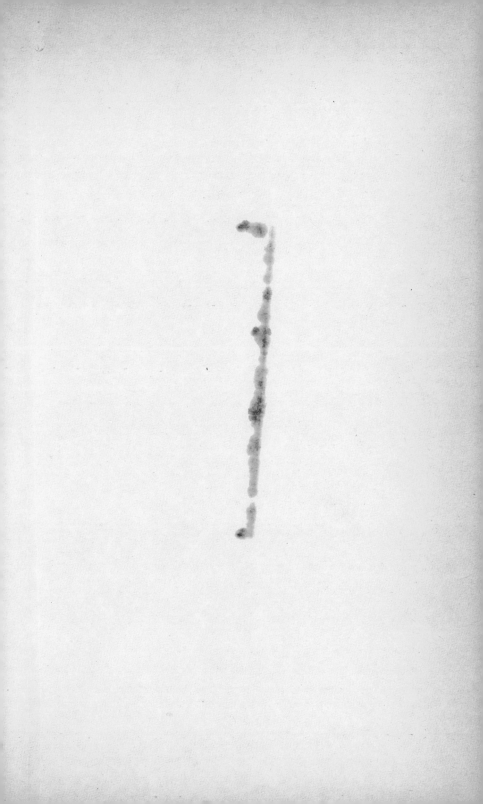